INSPIRATIONS
BRIDAL

COUNTRY BUMPKIN PUBLICATIONS

INSPIRATIONS BRIDAL

The breathtaking hand embroidered projects on the following pages are the perfect way to add a touch of romance and splendour to your wedding celebration or as a precious gift of love. They are destined to become the heirlooms of our daughters and granddaughters.
A toast to brides everywhere.

Sue Gardner,
Editor

CONTENTS

4
LOVE
An ivory pure silk bodice richly decorated in reds and golds

10
SERENITY
A beautiful garter made of pure white voile

12
ROMANCE
Superb horseshoe with apricot silk roses

14
KEEPSAKE
Gorgeous drawstring bag, garter and horseshoe

22
HARMONY
A stunning trio of heart, horseshoe and garter

MADE WITH LOVE

30
PEACE
Charming lingerie bag with an embroidered heart

36
CHERISH
Magical lace edged bag decorated with lily of the valley

40
ETERNITY
Opulent silk wedding ring cushion

50
BELOVED
Timeless stumpwork bridal bag

62
BLISS
Exquisite circular handbag mirror

68
DESIGNS OF THE HEART
A series of endearing designs perfect for your trousseau

77
ANGELS OF LOVE

80
ACKNOWLEDGEMENTS

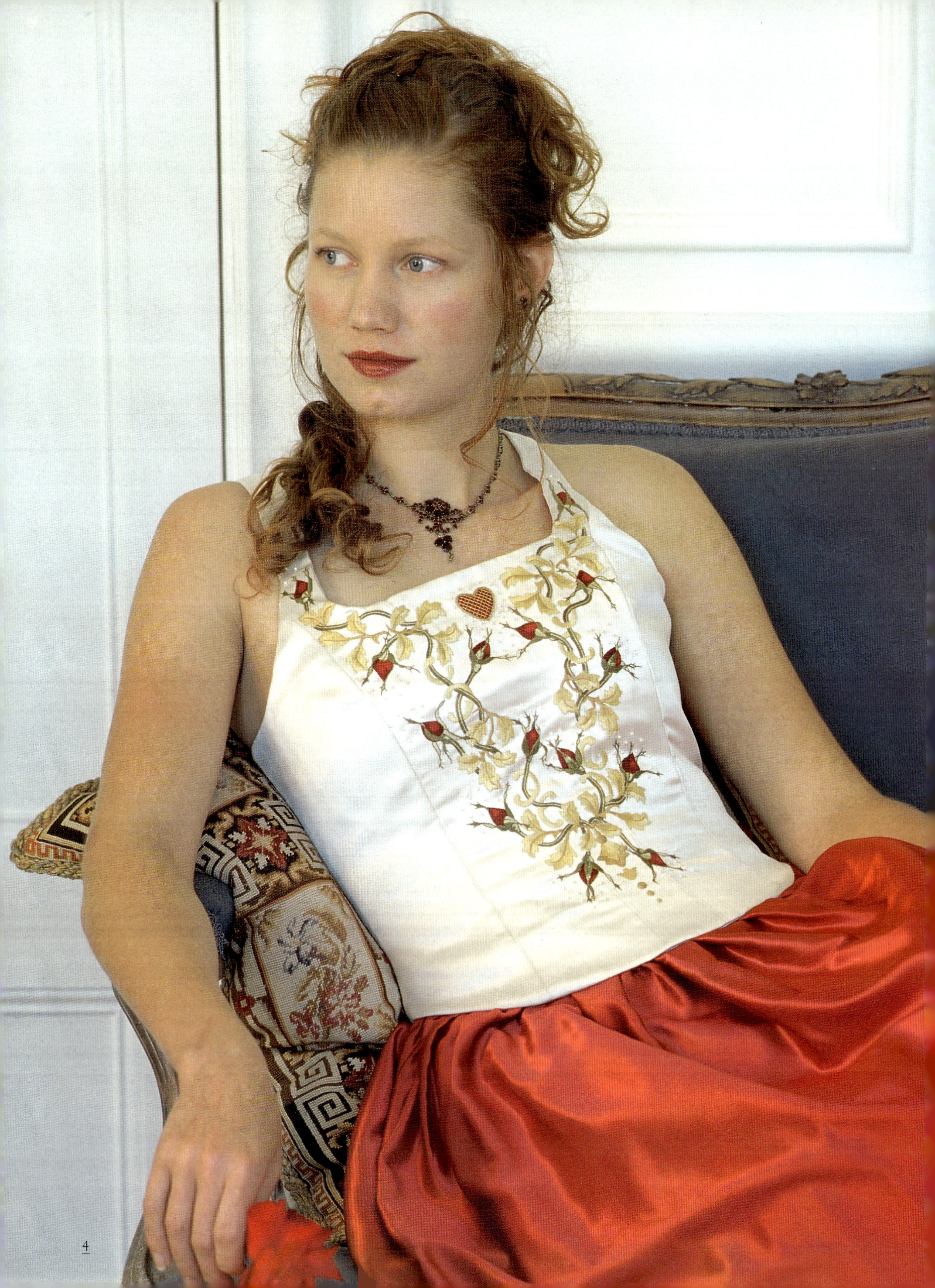

LOVE

An ivory pure silk bodice, strewn with lush golden leaves and deep red rosebuds. Glorious, passionate - for the most beautiful woman in the world. By Susan O'Connor of Victoria

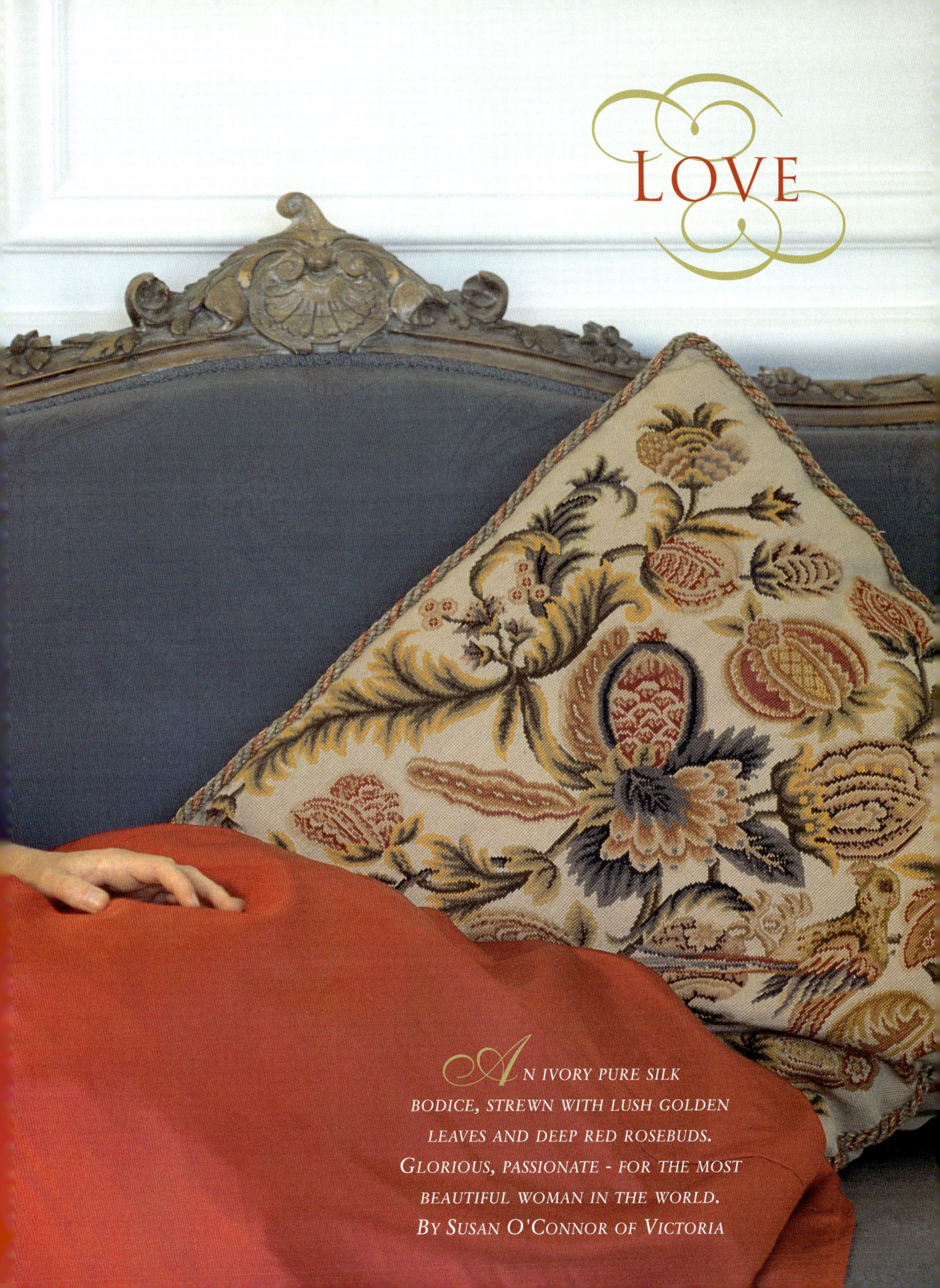

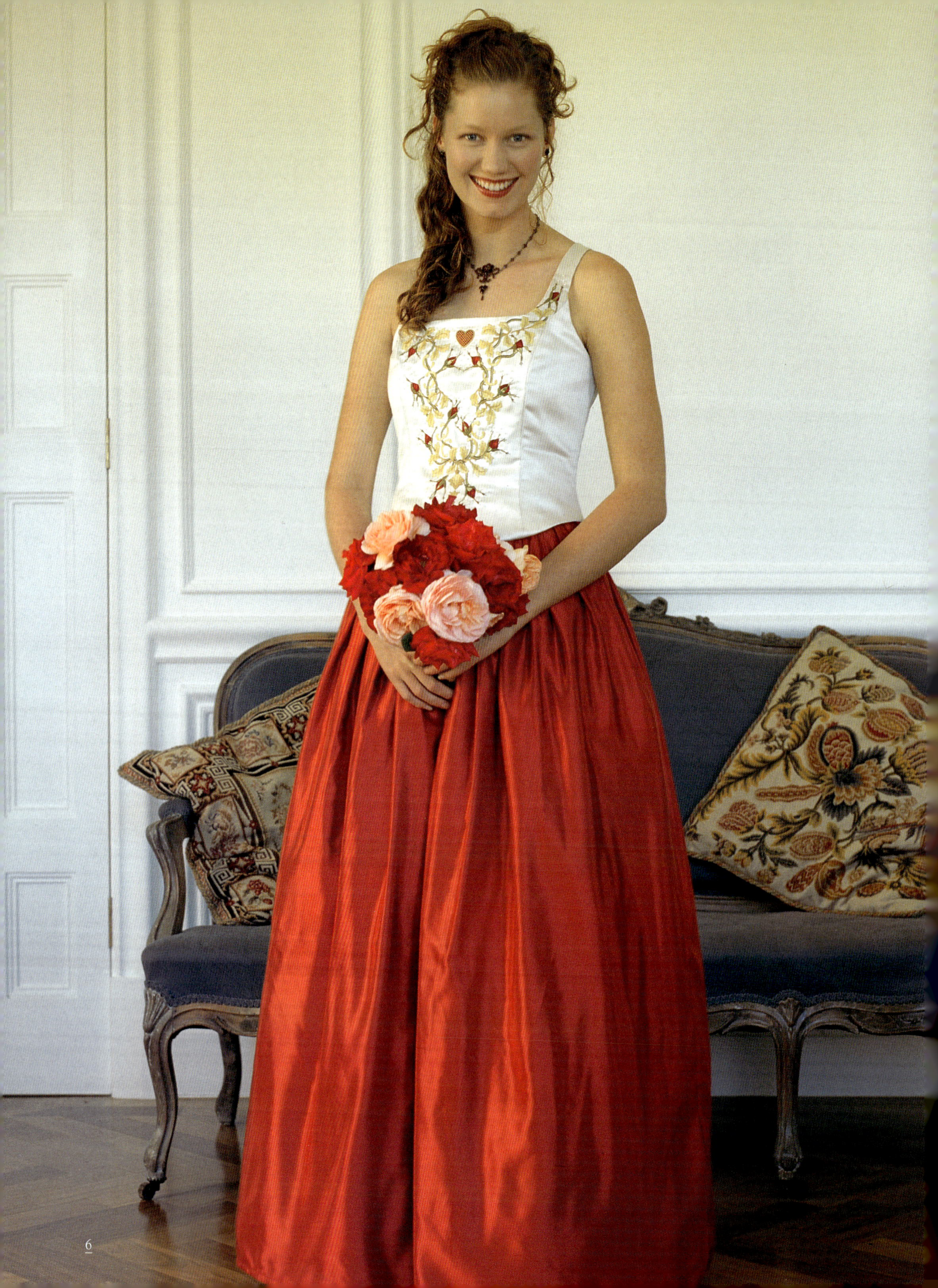

*...SHE WAS LIKE THE GIRL IN THE FAIRY STORY WHOSE WORDS
TURNED TO PEARLS AS THEY FELL FROM HER LIPS.*
L.P. HARTLEY - THE GO-BETWEEN

This glorious silk satin bodice is richly decorated with dark red rosebuds twining through ornate gold leaves. A padded heart is surrounded with whipped chain stitch and covered in a net of gold. Padded satin stitch spots and tiny pearls complete the design.

THIS DESIGN USES

*Beading, Blanket stitch, Lattice couching
Long and short blanket stitch
Long and short stitch, Padded satin stitch
Satin Stitch, Split stitch, Stem stitch
Straight stitch, Whipped chain stitch*

REQUIREMENTS

Sizes 10, 12 and 14

Fabric
80cm x 112cm wide (31 1/2" x 44") cream silk satin

Threads, Beads & Needle
See page 9.

Supplies
80cm x 112cm wide (31 1/2" x 44") woven interfacing (eg *Shapewell*)
80cm x 112cm wide (31 1/2" x 44") cream silk habutai for lining
5cm x 10cm wide (2" x 4") piece of red felt
3.4m x 12mm wide (3yd 26" x 1/2") white polyboning
50cm (20") white hook and eye tape
Matching silk machine sewing thread
Tracing paper
Wax free transfer paper (eg *Saral*)
Sharp lead pencil

PREPARATION FOR EMBROIDERY

See the liftout pattern for the pattern, cutting layouts, embroidery design and heart templates.

Preparing the front

Cut out all pattern pieces from both the silk satin and interfacing. Stitch the interfacing to the silk just outside the seam line on each piece. Trim away the interfacing within the seam allowance.

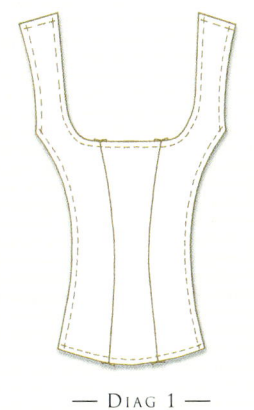

Pin and stitch the middle front sections to the centre front section *(diag 1)*. Clip the seams where necessary and press open.

Transferring the design

Trace the embroidery design and placement marks onto the tracing paper with the lead pencil. Lay the prepared fabric piece onto a hard surface. Place the transfer paper, face down, onto the right side of the fabric. Align the placement marks on the tracing with the centre front and upper edge of the bodice. Pin the papers in place, only pinning in the seam allowances. Pinning the transfer paper will leave visible marks.

Pressing firmly, trace over all design lines with the lead pencil. Remove the tracing and the transfer paper.

— DIAG 1 —

LOVE

STORING AND CARING FOR YOUR EMBROIDERY

After the happiness and excitement of a wedding, you may wish to preserve the precious mementos of this wonderful day. Care must be taken as items that are incorrectly stored can deteriorate over time and there is nothing more disappointing than finding your treasures damaged and discoloured. Before storing, ensure that items are clean. Any clothing should be professionally cleaned even if there are no obvious marks. This is especially important with silk as stains can develop over time, especially perspiration.

EMBROIDERY

All embroidery is worked with the sharp needle.

> *"Because the embroidery is not worked in a hoop, it is important to keep pressing the fabric so it remains flat. Place the embroidery, face down, onto a well padded surface. Lightly mist the back of the fabric with water and press with a steam iron."* SUSAN

Order of work

Outlines

Using one strand of light old gold thread, outline the gold leaves, stems, decorative curves, medallion, tulip shape and spots in split stitch. Outline the rosebuds and heart in the same manner using the raspberry thread and then the green stems and sepals using the medium olive green thread.

Leaves

Stitch the gold leaves and stems first, beginning with long and short blanket stitch and blanket stitch. Complete each leaf with long and short stitch and a stem stitch vein. Work the stems, decorative curves and tulip shape at the lower edge of the design in satin stitch. Embroider the padded satin stitch spots and medallion using all three shades of gold.

Rosebuds

Beginning with the darker shade, fill the rosebud shapes using the two shades of raspberry silk. Stitch the sepals and receptacles using the photograph as a guide to colour placement.

Finish the sepal tips with straight stitches. Fill the bud stems with rows of stem stitch.

Heart

Embroider the heart following the step-by-step instructions on page 10.

Pearls

The pearls are attached after the bodice has been constructed.

CONSTRUCTION

See the liftout pattern.

THREADS, BEADS & NEEDLE

Au Ver à Soie, Soie d'Alger stranded silk
A = 2132 lt olive green
B = 2134 med olive green
C = 2135 dk olive green
D = 2924 lt raspberry
E = 2925 raspberry

Madeira stranded silk
F = 2208 lt old gold
G = 2209 med old gold
H = 2210 dk old gold
I = cream pearl beads 2mm (1/16") wide

No. 12 sharp needle

EMBROIDERY KEY

All embroidery is worked with one strand of thread unless otherwise specified.

Gold foliage

Outlines = F (split stitch)

Leaves = F (long and short blanket stitch, blanket stitch), G (long and short stitch), H (stem stitch)

Stems = H (satin stitch)

Decorative curves = F (satin stitch)

Medallion = F (long and short stitch), G (long and short blanket stitch), H (blanket stitch)

Tulip shape = G (satin stitch)

Spots = F, G and H (padded satin stitch)

Rosebuds

Outlines = B and E (split stitch)

Buds = D and E (long and short stitch)

Sepals = A and C (satin stitch), B (satin stitch, straight stitch)

Receptacle = A, B and C (long and short stitch)

Stems = A, B and C (stem stitch)

Heart = E (split stitch, satin stitch), H (lattice couching; 2 strands, whipped chain stitch)

Pearls = I (beading)

STEP-BY-STEP HEART FOR LOVE

1. Work split stitch around the heart outline.

2. Cut two pieces of felt using the heart templates. Centre small heart within split stitch outline and secure with stab stitches.

3. Centre large felt heart over top of the first and attach in same manner. Embroider blanket stitches around the heart.

4. Work vertical satin stitches over the entire heart, covering the split stitch outline.

5. Work whipped chain stitch around the outer edge.

6. Work diagonal straight stitches, approx 3mm (1/8") apart, over the satin stitching.

7. Work diagonal straight stitches in the opposite direction, keeping them the same distance apart as before.

8. Work a tiny horizontal straight stitch at every point where two diagonal straight stitches cross. **Completed heart.**

SOMETHING BORROWED, SOMETHING BLUE...

SERENITY

*Delicate ribbon worked blue pansies on a lace edged garter.
Designed by Di Kirchner of South Australia*

REQUIREMENTS

Fabric & Lace

10cm x 92cm wide (4" x 36 1/4") piece of white voile

1.64m x 2cm wide (1yd 28 1/2" x 3/4") white lace edging

Supplies

Matching machine sewing thread

34cm x 13mm wide (13 3/8" x 1/2") white non roll elastic

10cm (4") square of medium weight interfacing

Sharp lead pencil

Ribbons, Beads & Needles

See opposite page.

CONSTRUCTION

See the liftout pattern.

The garter is completely assembled before the embroidery is attached.

PREPARATION FOR EMBROIDERY

Cut a 10cm (4") square of white voile and fuse the square of interfacing to the wrong side. Place a ruler across the centre of the square. Using the sharp lead pencil, make three dots 1.5cm (5/8") apart. These dots mark the positions of the centres of the ribbon pansies.

God, the best maker of all marriages, Combine your heart in one.
WILLIAM SHAKEPEARE

SERENITY... A BEAUTIFUL GARTER MADE OF PURE WHITE VOILE, STUDDED WITH MINIATURE PEARL BEADS.

EMBROIDERY

See page 49 for step-by-step instructions for working the ruched ribbon pansies.

The ribbon embroidery is stitched onto a piece of base fabric before being sewn onto the garter.

Use the no. 18 chenille needle when working with the 7mm (5/16") ribbon and the no. 22 needle for the 4mm (3/16") ribbon. Use the milliner's needle for attaching the beads and gathering the ribbon for the pansies.

Order of work

Pansies

Cut six pieces of blue silk ribbon, each 3cm (1 1/4") long for the upper petals and three pieces, each 8.5cm (3 3/8") long for the lower and middle petals. Fashion the petals following the instructions on page 49.

Secure a pansy to one marked dot on the fabric using tiny stab stitches around the centre.

THIS DESIGN USES

Beading, Loop stitch, Ruching

Attach a cluster of three pearl beads for the centre. Repeat for the remaining two pansies.

Ribbon loops

Using the green ribbon, work pairs of loop stitches, approximately 1.5cm (5/8") long, around the pansies. Start each loop under the pansy petals.

Change to the light pansy ribbon and embroider a pair of loop stitches above each pansy. Work single loop stitches between the pansies at the lower edge.

Cream bow

At each end of the spray, work two loop stitches approximately 2cm (3/4") long for the bow loops.

Embroider two loop stitches approximately 6cm (2 3/8") long below the middle pansy. Cut the loops at the end to form the ties of the bow. Trim the end of each tie at an angle to prevent fraying.

Finishing

Trim the excess fabric from around the embroidery. Centre the embroidery on the garter. Secure with several hand stitches at the upper and lower edges of the fabric near the middle.

RIBBONS, BEADS & NEEDLES

Kacoonda hand dyed silk ribbon 4mm (3/16") wide

A = 50cm (20") no. 5 lt pansy

YLI silk ribbon 4mm (3/16") wide

B = 60cm (24") no. 156 cream

YLI silk ribbon 7mm (5/16") wide

C = 50cm (20") no. 125 powder blue

Kacoonda hand dyed silk ribbon 7mm (5/16") wide

D = 60cm (24") no. 8E lt olive

Mill Hill glass seed beads

E = 02001 pearl

No. 9 milliner's (straw) needle
No. 18 chenille needle
No. 22 chenille needle

EMBROIDERY KEY

Pansies = C (ruching), E (beading)
Loops = A and D (loop stitch)
Cream bow = B (loop stitch)

ROMANCE

A superb horseshoe designed by Di Kirchner of South Australia

Any bride would love to carry this delightful good luck symbol on her wedding day. Pretty apricot silk roses are stitched onto gathered white voile and linked by a narrow band of white satin ribbon. Rosebuds and tiny gold beads surround each rose on the lace edged horseshoe. The finished horseshoe measures 19cm x 18cm wide (7 1/2" x 7 1/8").

This Design Uses

*Beading, Bullion knot, Detached chain
Fly stitch, Folded ribbon rose
Ribbon stitch, Straight stitch*

Requirements

Fabric

12cm x 90cm wide (4 3/4" x 35 1/2") piece of white cotton voile

Threads, Ribbons, Beads & Needles

See this page.

Supplies

90cm x 2cm wide (35 1/2" x 3/4") white cotton lace edging

1.8cm x 3mm wide (2yd" x 1/8") white satin ribbon

18cm (7 1/8") square of heavy card or plastic

18cm x 36cm wide (7 1/8" x 14 1/4") piece of wadding

Tracing paper

Sharp lead pencil

Construction

See the liftout pattern.

The horseshoe is completely assembled before the embroidery is worked.

Embroidery

Use the no. 10 milliner's needle for constructing the folded ribbon roses, thread embroidery and beading. Use the chenille needle for the ribbon embroidery.

Order of work

Roses

Cut the pink ribbon into seven 14cm (5 1/2") lengths. Fashion the folded ribbon roses.

Using matching thread, stitch a rose to the satin ribbon on the marked dots. Work the ribbon stitch leaves.

Rosebuds

Stitch the bullion buds, working both stitches through the same two holes in the fabric. Work two straight stitches at the tip of each bud and a fly stitch calyx which envelops the bullion knots.

Leaves

Using the khaki thread, complete the ribbon leaves by working a straight stitch which begins at the base and extends past the tip of each ribbon stitch. Work two fly stitches each side of the ribbon roses, close to the white satin ribbon.

Beaded flowers

Stitch five gold beads around each rose spray, using the photograph as a guide for placement. Work a detached chain around each bead beginning at the point closest to the rose. Work a straight stitch from the end of the detached chain to finish beneath the ribbon rose.

Bows

Cut two pieces of white satin ribbon, each 40cm (15 3/4") long. Tie each one into a bow. Using matching thread, stitch a bow onto each end of the horseshoe, concealing the end of the ribbon band. Attach a gold bead to the centre of each bow.

Threads, Ribbons, Beads & Needles

Anchor stranded cotton

A = 842 vy lt khaki green

DMC stranded cotton

B = 676 lt old gold

C = 819 lt baby pink

Kacoonda hand dyed silk ribbon 4mm (3/16") wide

D = 1m (39 1/2") no. 8J lt fern green

YLI silk ribbon 7mm (5/16") wide

E = 1m (39 1/2") no. 110 vy lt shell pink

Mill Hill glass seed beads

F = 00557 old gold

No. 10 milliner's (straw) needle

No. 22 chenille needle

Embroidery Key

All thread embroidery is worked with one strand unless otherwise specified.

Roses = E
(folded ribbon rose)

Rosebuds

Petals = C (2 strands, 2 bullion knots, 10 wraps)

Calyx = A (fly stitch)

Tip = A (straight stitch)

Leaves

Large leaves = D (ribbon stitch), A (straight stitch)

Small leaves = A (fly stitch)

Beaded flowers = F (beading), B (detached chain, straight stitch)

A GORGEOUS SILKEN DRAWSTRING POUCH
ENCRUSTED WITH PEARLS
DESIGNED BY HELEN ERIKSSON OF SOUTH AUSTRALIA

KEEPSAKE

~ GIFTS THAT SPEAK OF LOVE ~

For unrivalled romance, Helen has designed a glorious matching set of a bridal bag, horseshoe and garter. Romantic gypsophila and roses adorn the beautiful garter and horseshoe. The soft cream and ivory shades are accentuated with dainty pearls and crystals.

The exquisite bag complements the horseshoe and garter. Pearls and crystals highlight the silk ribbon flowers, which are worked onto purchased lace motifs. The design of the bag itself is simple but effective with elegant embroidered petals and pearl encrusted ends on the cord.

REQUIREMENTS

Fabric

14cm x 105cm wide (5 1/2" x 41 1/4") piece of cream silk dupion for garter

14cm x 105cm wide (5 1/2" x 41 1/4") piece of cream silk dupion for horseshoe

50cm x 105cm wide (20" x 41 1/4") piece of cream silk dupion for bag

80cm x 105cm wide (31 1/2" x 41 1/4") piece of cream silk dupion for all three items

Threads, Ribbons, Beads & Needles

See page 20.

Supplies

Beading thread (eg *Nymo*)

14cm (5 1/2") square of cardboard or plastic for horseshoe

10.5cm diameter (4 1/8") circle of cardboard or plastic for base of bag

1.5m x 7mm wide (1yd 23" x 5/16") double-sided cream satin ribbon for horseshoe

40cm x 2cm wide (15 3/4" x 3/4") non-roll elastic for garter

4 tea dyed guipure lace motifs each 12cm x 5cm wide (4 3/4" x 2") for bag

6 x 6mm (1/4") crystal beads for base of bag

Clear nylon thread

Tracing paper

Sharp lead pencil

CONSTRUCTION

See the liftout pattern.

The garter and horseshoe are completely assembled before the embroidery is worked.

PREPARATION FOR EMBROIDERY

See the liftout pattern for the embroidery designs.

Transferring the designs

Garter

Trace the embroidery design, including the placement marks, onto tracing paper. Centre the tracing over the completed garter, aligning the placement marks with the casing stitch lines. Pin in place to prevent movement. Using a large needle, pierce the tracing at the centre of each rose and at the ends of the design. Dot each hole with the lead pencil. Remove the tracing.

Horseshoe

Transfer the embroidery designs to the front of the completed horseshoe in the same manner as the garter.

Bag

Trace the embroidery design and petal shaping onto the tracing paper with a black pen. Cut out the petal fronts. Place the tracing over one petal, aligning the marked petal shaping with the raw edges of the fabric. Using the lead pencil, mark the position of the lace motif and the gypsophila sprays. Repeat for the remaining three petals.

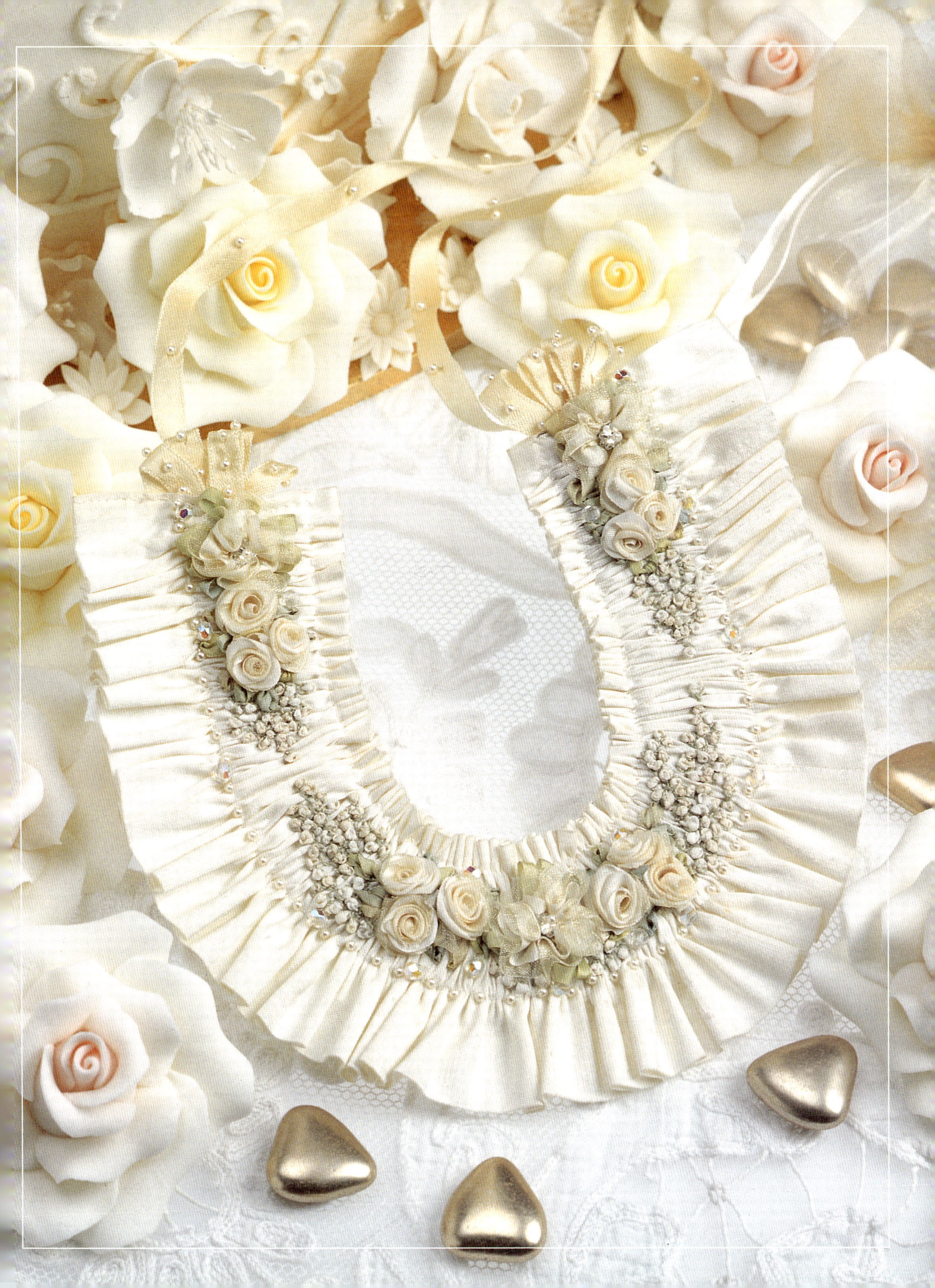

Keepsake

The Bag

Horseshoe (detail)

The Garter

Horseshoe (back)

18

EMBROIDERY

See page 21 for step-by-step instructions for creating the gathered ribbon roses.

Use the chenille needle when embroidering with the ribbon and the beading needle for attaching the beads. The crewel needle is used for making and securing the roses and for all other thread embroidery.

As the stitches should not be visible on the back of the garter and horseshoe, skim the needle between the fabric and elastic or cardboard. Finish off threads and ribbons on the front where they will be hidden by other embroidery or among the folds of the fabric.

The roses are made before they are attached to the fabric.

Garter

Gathered rose

Cut 18cm (7 1/8") of both C and F. Fashion a gathered ribbon rose following the instructions on page 21. Secure to the centre dot.

Folded roses

Cut 20cm (8") of both C and G. Using the two ribbons together as if they were one, form a folded ribbon rose. Make a second rose in exactly the same manner. Attach one rose on each side of the gathered rose.

Leaves

Using the green silk ribbon, tie a knot at one end and cut off the excess tail. Bring the needle up under a rose to hide the knot. Work loop stitches around the centre rose and detached chains around the side roses. Do this in a random fashion until the desired look is achieved.

Gypsophila sprays

Use the narrow cream silk ribbon to work sprays of French knots. Again, it is important not to take the needle through to the back. When starting, hide the knot among the gathers. Before pulling the needle through the French knot, bring it up at the position of the next knot, rather than to the back of the garter. Hold the knot firmly while pulling the needle through. To maintain the elasticity, do not pull the ribbon or thread too firmly as you move from one flower to the next.

Partially surround each French knot with a fly stitch for the foliage.

Crystals and pearls

Attach six crystals around the centre rose. Add a cluster of three pearl beads 2cm (3/4") from each end of the gypsophila sprays.

Horseshoe

Gathered roses

Make five gathered roses following the instructions on page 21. Secure three roses to the front of the horseshoe at the marked positions. The remaining two roses are attached to the back of the horseshoe and cover the ends of the ribbon loops.

Gathered roses

Make four gathered roses following the instructions on page 21. Secure a rose to each lace motif at the position shown on the photograph. Surround each one with loop stitch leaves.

Folded roses

Make four folded roses in the same manner as those for the garter. Attach a rose to each lace motif at the position shown on the photograph. Surround each one with detached chain leaves.

Gypsophila sprays

Embroider the sprays of gypsophila following the garter instructions.

Crystals and pearls

Using the photograph as a guide to placement, attach pearl beads and crystals to the lace motifs except for the unattached sections at the lower edge.

THESE DESIGNS USE

*Beading, Detached chain, Fly stitch
Folded ribbon rose, French knot
Gathered ribbon rose, Loop stitch*

Folded roses

Make twelve folded ribbon roses in the same manner as those on the garter. Attach the roses, in groups of three, at the marked positions.

Leaves

Stitch the leaves in the same manner as for the garter.

Gypsophila sprays

Work the sprays of gypsophila following the instructions for those on the garter.

Crystals and pearls

Attach pearl beads and crystals along the lower stitch line of the casing. Position the pearls at approximately 7mm (5/16") intervals and the crystals at approximately 3.5cm (1 3/8") intervals. Add crystals near the clusters of folded roses at the positions indicated on the design.

Bag

Lace motifs

Pin the lace motifs to the right side of the petals at the position indicated on the pattern. Using the invisible sewing thread, secure the motifs in place, leaving 2.5cm (1") at the lower end unattached.

THREADS, RIBBONS, BEADS & NEEDLES

Anchor stranded cotton
A = 858 lt fern green
B = 926 ultra lt beige

Kacoonda hand dyed silk ribbon 7mm (5/16") wide
C = 4 cream

Kacoonda hand dyed silk ribbon 4mm (3/16") wide
D = 4 cream
E = 8J lt fern green

Mokuba no.1500 organdy ribbon 11mm (3/8") wide
F = 12 cream

Mokuba no. 1500 organdy ribbon 5mm (3/16") wide
G = 12 cream

H = diamante flowers
6mm (1/4") wide

I = crystal beads
4mm (3/16") wide

J = cream pearl beads
2mm (1/16") wide

No. 9 crewel needle

No. 13 beading needle

No. 20 chenille needle

EMBROIDERY KEY

All thread embroidery is worked with two strands.

Gathered roses

Petals = C and F
(gathered ribbon rose),
B (attaching)

Centre = H and J (beading)

Leaves = E (loop stitch)

Folded roses

Petals = C and G (folded ribbon rose), B (attaching)

Leaves = E (detached chain)

Gypsophila

Flowers = D
(French knot, 1 wrap)

Foliage = A (fly stitch)

Ribbon & Bead Requirements

	Garter	Horseshoe	Bag
C	60cm (23 5/8")	3.4m (3yd 26")	1.6m (1yd 27")
D	1.5m (1yd 23")	3m (3yd 10")	2.5m (2yd 26")
E	1.5m (1yd 23")	3m (3yd 10")	4.5m (4yd 33 1/4")
F	20cm (8")	1m (39 1/2")	80cm (31 1/2")
G	40cm (16")	2.4m (2yd 22 1/2")	80cm (31 1/2")
H	1	7	4
I	6	17	44

~ The finished bag measures 16.5cm high x 14cm in diameter (6 1/2" x 5 1/2").

~ The finished horseshoe measures 17cm square (6 3/4").

~ The garter measures 6cm x 38cm in diameter (2 3/8" x 15").

Step-by-step Gathered Ribbon Rose

1. Cut 18cm (7") of both C and F. Place the silk ribbon on top of the organdy ribbon.

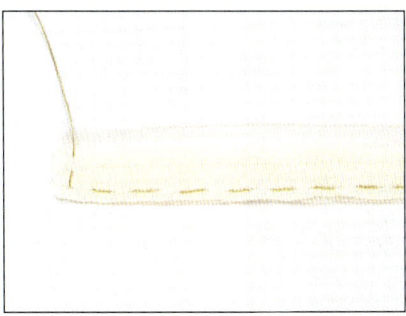

2. Stitch across one end, along one long edge and up the other end with small running stitches.

3. Pull the thread tight to gather the ribbon into a flower shape.

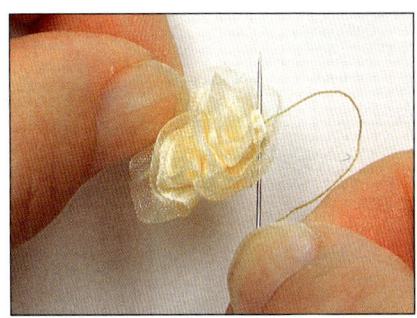

4. To hold the gathers, work two or three tiny stitches through both ends of the ribbon.

5. Attach the gathered ribbon to the fabric with tiny stitches around the centre.

6. Bring the thread up through the centre of the rose. Slip a flower diamanté and then a pearl bead onto the needle.

7. Take the needle back through the diamanté only.

8. Finish off with tiny back stitches in the folds of the ribbon. **Completed gathered ribbon rose.**

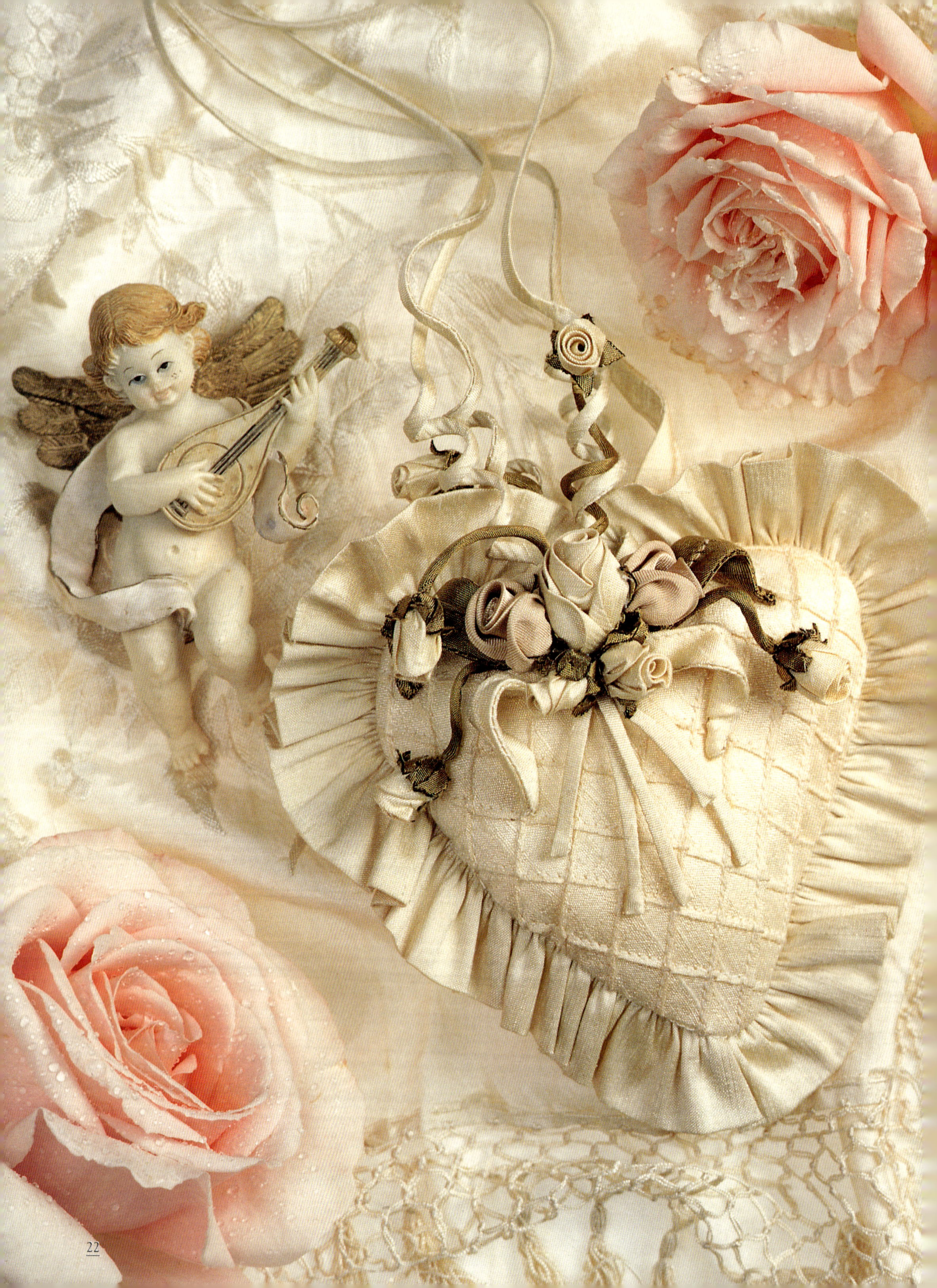

Only the soul that loves is happy ~ GOETHE

A STUNNING TRIO OF HEART, HORSESHOE AND GARTER

~ HARMONY ~

BY ELINA AKSELROD OF VICTORIA

~ HARMONY ~

Elegant roses and buds, fashioned from silk dupion and silk satin, decorate the front of this traditional garter, horseshoe and heart. The leaves, also made from silk fabric, feature pintucks for the centre veins. A lattice of pintucks decorates the front of the horseshoe and heart. The horseshoe and heart are suspended from fine rouleaux.

Construction

See the liftout pattern.

The heart, horseshoe and garter are completely assembled before the floral sprays are attached.

Preparation

See the liftout pattern for the patterns, placement marks, cutting layouts and templates.

Preparing the fabric for the roses, leaves and rouleaux

Cut out all the pieces of fabric for the roses and buds. These are cut on the bias. Cut out the leaves, sepals and the bias strips for the rouleaux.

Assembling the Floral Sprays

See pages 27 - 29 for step-by-step instructions for making a rolled rose, rosebud, pintucked leaf and rouleaux.

Make all roses, rosebuds, leaves and rouleaux following the instructions on pages 27 - 29. Use the photograph as a guide for positioning the roses, rosebuds and leaves.

The Garter ~

THE FINISHED GARTER MEASURES 6.5CM X 33CM IN CIRCUMFERENCE (2 5/8" X 13").

Rosebuds and tendrils

Cut the piece of wire into five equal lengths. Cut the green rouleau into three equal lengths and thread onto three pieces of the wire for the stems.

These Designs Use

Gathering, Granitos, Pintucks Rolled roses, Rouleau

The remaining pieces of wire are for the tendrils.

Work a rosebud around the end of one stem and secure to the stem with tiny back stitches. Place a small amount of craft glue around the base of the bud and attach 5 - 6 sepals. Bend the top of each sepal over so it sits away from the bud. Form a slight twist in the stem and attach to the garter with tiny hand stitches. Repeat for the remaining two rosebuds.

For the tendrils, cut two pieces of cream rouleau to fit the remaining pieces of wire. Place the wire inside the rouleau and turn one raw end to the inside. Neaten with tiny slip stitches.

Wrap each tendril around a pencil or knitting needle to form a spiral. Stitch in place near the top of the design.

Dangling rouleaux

Cut the remaining length of cream rouleau into seven pieces of varying lengths. Neaten one end of each piece in the same manner as the stems.

Lay each rouleau side by side near the centre of the design, with the longer pieces in the middle and the shorter ones either side. Attach them to the garter with tiny hand stitches.

Leaves

Make two small green and two small cream leaves. Stitch the base of each leaf to the garter.

Make a fold in each leaf, pushing them towards the centre of the design. Secure the fold and the tip with 2 - 3 invisible stitches. This fold is made to prevent the leaf from overstretching when the garter is worn.

Roses

Make two cream roses, two beige roses and one ecru rose. Place the two cream roses over the leaves, rosebuds and tendrils in a north and south position, followed by the two beige roses, placing these in an east and west position. Stitch the base of each rose in place.

Using tiny back stitches, attach 5 - 6 sepals around the base of the ecru rose.

Secure the ecru rose to the centre of the design with small stitches, keeping them as invisible as possible.

Finishing

To ensure the roses stay in place, add extra stitches where necessary, keeping them as invisible as possible.

The Horseshoe ~

THE HORSESHOE MEASURES 16CM X 14CM WIDE (6 3/8" X 5 1/2").

Rosebuds

Cut two pieces of wire, each 7cm (2 3/4") long and one piece 5cm (2") long.

~ FOLLOW YOUR HEART ~

Make three ecru rosebuds on stems in the same manner as for the garter.

Form a slight twist in the stem and attach the short stemmed rosebud to the top of the design and a long stemmed rosebud on each side.

Using the cream fabric, make two more rosebuds without stems.

Leaves

Make two large green and three large cream leaves. Stitch the leaves to the design in the same manner as those on the garter.

Roses

Make two cream roses, two ecru roses and two beige roses. Place the two cream roses on the design in a north and south position, followed by the two beige roses in an east and west position. Stitch the base of each rose in place.

Secure the two ecru roses in place at the centre of the design.

Finishing

To ensure the roses stay in place, add extra stitches where necessary, keeping them as invisible as possible.

The Heart ~

THE FINISHED HEART MEASURES 16CM X 14CM WIDE (6 3/8" X 5 1/2").

Spots

On the back of the heart, work a row of granitos spots around the outer edge at approximately 1cm (3/8") intervals. Work each one with 7 - 8 straight stitches.

Handles

Make two rouleaux, each 70cm (27 1/2") long. Cut four pieces of wire, each 8cm (3 1/8") long. Push a piece of wire into the end of one rouleau. Holding the end, wrap the wired section around a pencil or knitting needle. Repeat with the other three pieces of wire and rouleau ends.

Attach the ends of one rouleau to the front of the heart. Attach the ends of the remaining piece to the back in the same manner.

Hanging rouleaux

Cut the remaining rouleau into five pieces of varying lengths. Turn in one end of each length and slip stitch closed. Secure the raw ends to the heart front with small hand stitches.

Rosebuds

Cut the piece of wire and the length of green rouleau into two pieces, each 10cm (4") long and four pieces, each 6cm (2 3/8") long. Make the stems as for the garter.

Work a rosebud around the end of each stem and form a slight twist in the stem. Attach four rosebuds to the front of the heart and two to the back. Make four rosebuds without stems.

Leaves

Make two small green leaves, three small cream leaves and one large cream leaf.

Stitch two green and two small cream leaves to the front of the heart. On the back of the heart, attach one small and one large cream leaf. Secure the tip of the large leaf to the rouleau handle near the top of the spiral.

Roses and rosebuds

Make two beige roses and one ecru rose. Attach sepals around the three roses. Place the roses on the front of the design and stitch in place.

Attach two of the remaining cream rosebuds to the design just under the roses and over the hanging rouleaux. Attach the last two rosebuds to the back of the heart over the ends of the handles.

Making a collage of your mementos

One lovely way of storing wedding mementos, which also allows you to enjoy them, is to have a collage of objects arranged and framed. This can include anything from horseshoes to confetti but take care to properly frame and use only acid free card. A little care taken when storing precious objects will ensure that you can enjoy them for many years to come.

Note: if making all three pieces the following fabric amounts are required

A = 80cm x 112cm wide (31 1/2" x 44") piece of cream silk dupion

B = 20cm x 95cm wide (8" x 37 1/2") piece of ecru silk dupion

C = 25cm x 90cm wide (10" x 35 1/2") piece of green silk satin

D = 20cm x 112cm wide (8" x 44") piece of beige silk satin

20cm x 28cm wide (8" x 11") piece of paper-backed fusible web (eg *Vliesofix*)

The Heart ~

Requirements

Fabric

A = 45cm x 90cm wide (18" x 35 1/2") piece of cream silk dupion

B = 15cm x 35cm wide (6" x 14") piece of ecru silk dupion

C = 25cm x 30cm wide (10" x 12") piece of green silk satin

D = 15cm x 35cm wide (6" x 14") piece of beige silk satin

Thread & Needle

Anchor stranded cotton

E = 885 vanilla

No. 9 crewel needle

Supplies

Small amount of polyester fibre-fill

28cm x 14cm wide (11" x 5 1/2") piece of paper-backed fusible web (eg *Vliesofix*)

90cm (35 1/2") x 20 gauge wire

Water soluble fabric marker

Matching machine sewing threads

Embroidery Key

Centre rose = B

Side roses = D

Rosebuds = A

Sepals and stems = C

Large leaves = A and C

Small leaves = A and C

Handles = A

The Horseshoe ~

Requirements

Fabric

A = 45cm x 112cm wide (18" x 44") piece of cream silk dupion

B = 15cm x 35cm wide (6" x 14") piece of ecru silk dupion

C = 20cm x 30cm wide (8" x 12") piece of green silk satin

D = 15cm x 35cm wide (6" x 14") piece of beige silk satin

Needle

No. 9 crewel needle

Supplies

20cm (8") square of thin wadding (eg *Pellon*)

14cm (5 1/2") square of paper-backed fusible web (eg *Vliesofix*)

40cm (15 3/4") x 20 gauge wire

15cm x 12cm wide (6" x 5") piece of cardboard or plastic

Craft glue

Water soluble fabric marker

Matching machine sewing threads

Embroidery Key

Centre roses = B

Side roses = D

Upper and lower roses = A

Rosebuds = A and B

Sepals and stems = C

Large leaves = A and C

Handles = A

The Garter ~

Requirements

Fabric

A = 40cm x 100cm wide (15 3/4" x 39 1/2") piece of cream silk dupion

B = 15cm x 25cm wide (6" x 10") piece of ecru silk dupion

C = 20cm x 30cm wide (8" x 12") piece of green silk satin

D = 15cm x 35cm wide (6" x 14") piece of beige silk satin

Needle

No. 9 crewel needle

Supplies

35cm (14") x 20 gauge wire

35cm x 2cm wide (13 3/4" x 3/4") non-roll elastic

14cm (5 1/2") square of paper-backed fusible web (eg *Vliesofix*)

Craft glue

Water soluble fabric marker

Matching machine sewing threads

Embroidery Key

Centre rose = B

Side roses = A and D

Rosebuds = A

Sepals and stems = C

Small leaves = A and C

Hanging rouleaux = A

Spirals of rouleaux = A

Back of heart

Marriages are made in heaven.
ALFRED, LORD TENNYSON

STEP-BY-STEP ROLLED ROSE

This rolled rose is made from silk dupion. The fabric is cut on the bias with each rose consisting of a rolled centre and two petals.

1. Centre. Fold one strip in half along the length and press. Fold the end over. Thread a needle and knot the thread.

2. Begin rolling folded end of strip firmly. Take 2 - 3 tiny back stitches through the base. Leave the thread dangling.

3. Continue rolling, taking 2 - 3 tiny stitches through the base after each roll.

4. When reaching the end, fold the tail of fabric backwards.

5. Secure with 2 - 3 back stitches. Take the needle through the base 2 - 3 more times. Leave thread dangling.

6. Outer petals. Fold a square of fabric in half diagonally and press.

7. Fold a small pleat at one side near the centre.

8. Repeat on the other side.

9. Make a second small pleat on each side.

10. Fold the ends to the back. Secure the folds with tiny back stitches. Make a second petal in the same manner.

11. Attaching petals. Place one petal around the base of the centre and stitch in place with tiny back stitches.

12. Place the second petal around the centre, overlapping the base of the first petal. Stitch in place.

13. Work a few more stitches through base of petals and centre to secure. Trim. **Completed rose.**

27

Love is, above all, the gift of oneself.
JEAN ANOUILH

STEP-BY-STEP PINTUCKED LEAF

1. Cut out two leaf shapes. With right sides together, stitch along both long sides, pivoting at the point.

2. Trim the seam allowance to 3mm (1/8"). Turn through to the right side and press.

3. Fold the leaf in half along the length.

4. Beginning at the base, stitch 1.5mm (1/16") from the fold. Run stitching off folded edge 1 - 2cm (3/8 - 3/4") from tip.

5. Take the tails of thread to the back and knot them.

6. Take tails inside leaf. Re-emerge and pull thread taut. Trim. The ends will retract inside leaf. **Completed leaf.**

STEP-BY-STEP ROULEAU

Cut the length of bias following the instructions in the centre liftout.

1. With right sides together, fold strip in half along length. Stitch 4mm (3/16") from folded edge.

2. Trim the seam allowance to 4mm (3/16").

3. Cut one end diagonally from stitch line to fold. Thread a large needle with strong thread. Knot ends. Secure through seam 1cm (3/8") from point.

4. Insert the needle into the tube and work it through the tube until it appears at the other end.

5. Gently pull on the thread to turn the tube right side out.

6. Cut the tube into the desired lengths. **Completed rouleau.**

STEP-BY-STEP STEMMED ROSEBUD

The rosebuds are worked in a similar manner to the roses, omitting one petal. For some, the centres are worked around a stem. Cut out the fabric for the centre of the rosebud. Cut out and make one petal following steps 6 - 10 for the rose.

1. Making the stem. Place the wire inside the rouleau tube. Overcast the ends to prevent the wire from slipping out.

2. Centre. Fold fabric strip in half and fold end back. Begin wrapping strip around stem 7mm (5/16") from end.

3. Secure the base to the stem with 2 - 3 tiny back stitches.

4. Continue wrapping and securing the centre until almost reaching the end.

5. Fold the end back and secure to the base and stem as before.

6. Outer petal. Using tiny back stitches, wrap the petal around base of the centre. Stitch in place. Trim excess fabric.

7. Sepals. Fuse a piece of fusible web onto the back of one piece of green silk satin.

8. Peel away the backing paper. Place the second piece of green silk satin over the web and fuse in place.

9. Transfer the sepal shapes to the fabric. Cut out the pieces of green fabric for the sepals.

10. Using a very small amount of craft glue, attach one sepal to the base of the bud, ensuring the end is on the stem.

11. Attach a second sepal in same manner, slightly overlapping the first. Continue attaching pieces until reaching the starting point.

12. Bend back the tip of each sepal and finger press. Form a slight twist in the stem. **Completed rosebud and stem.**

29

PEACE

A truly charming lingerie bag to store your treasures designed by Kris Richards of South Australia

Almost too pretty to keep in the drawer, this beautiful lingerie bag is created from subtly shaded moiré, overlaid with silk organza. Daintily embroidered sprays of roses are linked together to form a delicate heart shape. The top of the bag closes with a wide organza bow.

REQUIREMENTS

Fabric

35cm x 130cm wide (13 3/4" x 51") piece of ivory moiré

70cm x 135cm wide (27 5/8" x 53 1/8") ivory silk organza

Threads & Needles

See page 34.

Supplies

Fine tipped water soluble fabric marker

PREPARATION FOR EMBROIDERY

See the liftout pattern for the cutting layout and embroidery design.

Transferring the design

Following the cutting layout, cut the bag overlay from the organza.

Fold the organza in half across the width and mark the centre of the fold line with a pin *(diag 1)*. Unfold and measure up 6.5cm (2 1/2") from the pin. Using the fabric marker make a small dot at this position. This will be the lower tip of the heart shape.

Measure up a further 8.5cm (3 3/8") and mark again. This will be the position of the smaller granitos at the centre top of the heart.

Place the organza over the embroidery design, aligning the marks on the pattern with the dots on the fabric.

Using the fabric marker, trace the teardrop outlines and along the design lines for the vines. Mark the centre of each rose and spot with a dot.

Preparing the fabric

With the wrong side of the organza facing the right side of the moiré, place the two pieces together. Using a fine needle and thread, tack around the edges of the fabric and across the fold line. Work the rows of tacking following the diagram *(diag 2)*.

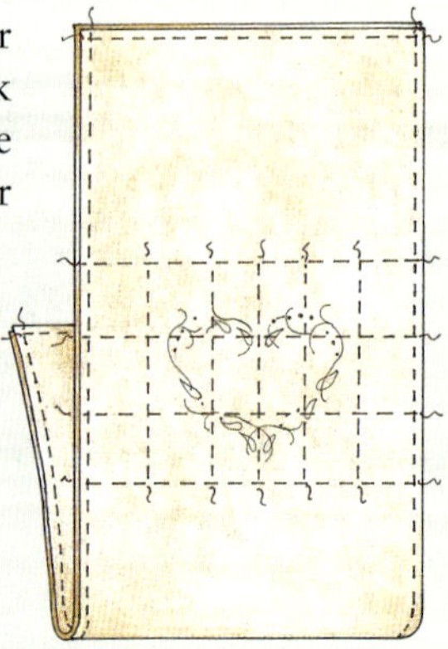

EMBROIDERY

Use the no. 7 milliner's needle for the bullion roses and the no. 9 milliner's needle for the bullion leaves and white daisies. The crewel needle is used for all other embroidery.

— DIAG 1 —

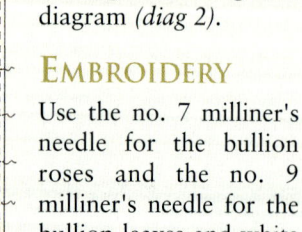

— DIAG 2 —

Order of work

Teardrops and spots

Outline one teardrop in stem stitch, then continue working rounds of stem stitch until it is filled. Complete all the other teardrops in the same manner. Add a granitos spot close to each teardrop and at the marked positions inside the heart.

Vines

Stitch the vines in stem stitch and add the leaves along them. Use two bullion knots for each leaf. Add a straight stitch that extends from the tip of the leaf to give a more elegant shape.

Large roses

Beginning at the centre, embroider a bullion knot with the darkest pink thread. Using the medium shade of pink, work 2 - 3 bullion knots for the inner petals. Stitch the remaining petals with the lightest pink thread, placing them around the lower edge and sides of the rose.

Small roses

Work the centre with a bullion knot in the darkest pink thread. Stitch two bullion knots for the inner petals. Surround these with overlapping bullion knots in the lightest pink thread for the outer petals.

Rosebuds

Embroider two bullion knots side by side for the tiny rosebuds at the ends of the sprays. Work two bullion knots at the base of each bud for the sepals.

Daisies

To embroider the white daisies, work two bullion knots for each petal and then add the French knot centres.

Scatter blue daisies among the roses, using the photograph as a guide for placement.

Leaves

Work the bullion leaves around the roses in the same manner as the vine leaves. Scatter detached chain leaves around the edges of each group of flowers.

Tiny buds

Using detached chains, embroider tiny pink buds around the roses.

CONSTRUCTION

See the liftout pattern.

THE FINISHED BAG MEASURES 53CM X 33CM WIDE (21" X 13").

Using natural remedies

Moths, beetles and silverfish are the lethal enemies of fabrics, so some form of repellant is required to keep them away. You may like to use natural remedies, such as cedar, as they impart a wonderful fragrance.

Alternatively there are numerous commercial products available but remember to refresh your repellant as required.

Threads & Needles

DMC stranded cotton

A = blanc
B = 223 lt shell pink
C = 224 vy lt shell pink
D = 225 ultra lt shell pink
E = 371 verdigris
F = 676 lt old gold
G = 744 lt yellow
H = 834 vy lt golden olive

I = 3032 putty groundings
J = 3053 green-grey
K = 3747 vy lt blue-violet

Madeira Decora stranded rayon

L = 1513 blush pink

No. 7 milliner's (straw) needle
No. 9 milliner's (straw) needle
No. 9 crewel needle

Embroidery Key

All embroidery is worked with one strand of thread unless otherwise specified.

Teardrops = H (stem stitch)

Spots = H (granitos)

Large roses

Centre = B (2 strands, bullion knot, 6 wraps)

Inner petals = C (2 strands, 2 - 3 bullion knots, 10 wraps)

Outer petals = D (2 strands, 4 - 6 bullion knots, 20 wraps)

Small roses

Centre = B (2 strands, bullion knot, 6 wraps)

Inner petals = C (2 strands, 2 - 3 bullion knots, 10 wraps)

Outer petals = D (2 strands, 3 bullion knots, 16 - 20 wraps)

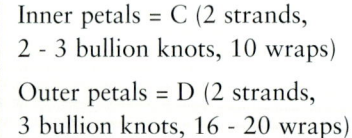

Rosebuds

Petals = C (2 strands, 2 bullion knots, 6 - 10 wraps)

Sepals = I (2 bullion knots, 8 - 10 wraps)

Tiny buds = L (detached chain)

This Design Uses

Bullion knot, Detached chain
French knot, Granitos
Stem stitch, Straight stitch

White daisies

Petals = A
(2 bullion knots, 10 wraps)

Centre = G (French knot, 1 wrap)

Blue daisies

Petals = K
(detached chain)

Centre = F (French knot, 1 wrap)

Leaves and vines

Rose leaves = I (2 bullion knots, 8 - 15 wraps, straight stitch)

Vines = J (stem stitch)

Vine leaves = J (2 bullion knots, 8 - 15 wraps, straight stitch)

Scattered leaves = E (detached chain)

STEP-BY-STEP BULLION KNOT

The distance between A and B is the length of the finished bullion knot. To form a straight knot the number of wraps must cover this distance. Add an extra 1 - 2 wraps to ensure they are tightly packed. More wraps are required to form a curved knot.

↑ indicates top of fabric

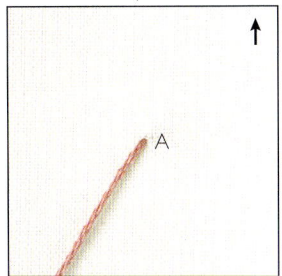

1. Bring the needle to the front at A. Pull the thread through.

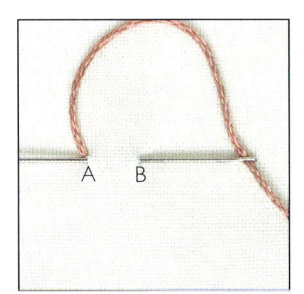

2. Take the needle to the back at B. Re-emerge at A, taking care not to split the thread. The thread is to the right of the needle.

3. Rotate the fabric. Raise the point of the needle away from the fabric. Wrap the thread clockwise around the needle.

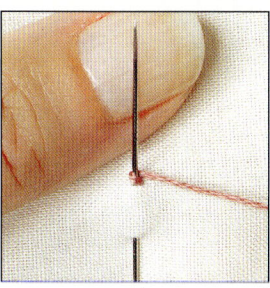

4. Keeping the point of the needle raised, pull the wrap firmly down onto the fabric.

5. Work the required number of wraps around the shaft of the needle. Pack them down evenly as you wrap.

6. Keeping tension on the wraps with the left thumb, begin to ease the needle through the fabric and wraps.

7. Continuing to keep tension on the wraps, pull the needle and thread through the wraps (thumb not shown).

8. Pull the thread all the way through, tugging it away from you until a small pleat forms in the fabric. This helps to ensure a tight even knot.

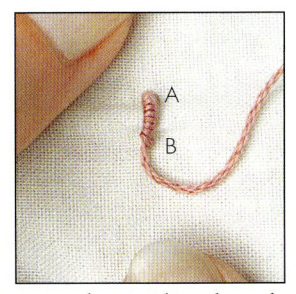

9. Release the thread. Smooth out the fabric and the knot will lay back towards B.

10. To ensure all the wraps are even, gently stroke and manipulate them with the needle while maintaining the tension on the thread.

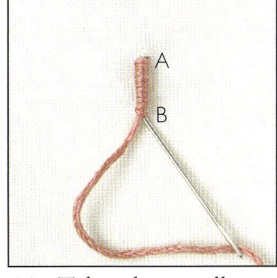

11. Take the needle to the back at B to anchor the knot.

12. Pull the thread through and end off. **Completed bullion knot.**

CHERISH

The understated perfection of a lily of the valley embroidered on delicate voile. Designed by Elina Akselrod of Victoria

~ DREAMS COME TRUE ~

This magical lace edged bag, decorated with a lily of the valley, can be filled with sweets, soap or something more precious as a lovely way of saying thank you to your bridesmaids or a special friend. The bag is made using two layers of fine cotton voile edged with cream cotton lace. The finished bag measures 18.5cm x 16cm wide (7 1/4" x 6 1/4").

REQUIREMENTS

Fabric & Lace

35cm x 40cm wide (13 3/4" x 15 3/4") piece of cream cotton voile

60cm x 2cm wide (24" x 3/4") cream cotton lace edging

76cm x 12mm wide (30" x 1/2") cream cotton lace edging

30cm x 2cm wide (12" x 3/4") cream cotton lace beading

Threads & Needle

See opposite page.

Supplies

76cm x 10mm wide (30" x 3/8") cream satin ribbon

10cm (4") embroidery hoop

Sharp lead pencil

Tracing paper

PREPARATION FOR EMBROIDERY

See the liftout pattern for the pattern and the embroidery design.

Preparing the tracing

Place a piece of tracing paper over the bag pattern. Using a black pen, trace the cutting lines for the front and the embroidery design.

THIS DESIGN USES

*Granitos, Padded satin stitch
Seed stitch, Shadow work, Stem stitch,
Straight stitch*

Transferring the design

With the right side of the fabric facing, place the fabric over the tracing. Pin in place to prevent movement. Using the lead pencil, trace the cutting lines and the embroidery design. Cut out the front and place in the hoop.

EMBROIDERY

See the opposite page for the step-by-step instructions for shadow work.

Order of work

Using the green thread, embroider the leaves in shadow work.

Work the two long flower stems next, followed by the two shorter ones.

Change to the ecru thread and embroider the flowers. Each large flower is stitched in padded satin stitch, while the flowers at the ends of the stems are worked with a granitos of 10 - 12 stitches. Attach each flower to the stem with a tiny straight stitch.

Single or pairs of seed stitches are worked under each of the flowers.

Scatter more tiny seed stitches around the design. Embroider a satin stitch ribbon around the stems and add two straight stitches on each side.

CONSTRUCTION

See the liftout pattern.

Threads & Needle

DMC stranded cotton

A = ecru

B = 523 lt fern green

C = 524 vy lt fern green

D = 739 ultra lt tan

No. 12 sharp needle

Embroidery Key

All embroidery is worked with two strands of thread unless otherwise specified.

Leaves = B (shadow work)

Stems = B (stem stitch)

Flowers = A (padded satin stitch, granitos), D (1 strand, seed stitch)

Flower stems = C (1 strand, straight stitch)

Ribbon = A (satin stitch, straight stitch)

Scattered spots = A (1 strand, seed stitch)

Sugared Almonds

A gift of five almonds represents health, wealth, long life, fertility and happiness. This wedding tradition dates back to the early days of European history.

Step-by-step shadow work

Shadow work creates a delicate effect of shading on fine fabrics. It can be worked from either side of the fabric. Here it is worked from the right side.

1. Begin with a waste knot. Bring needle to front at A, 1.5mm (1/16") from tip of shape. Pull through. Take needle to back at B, at tip.

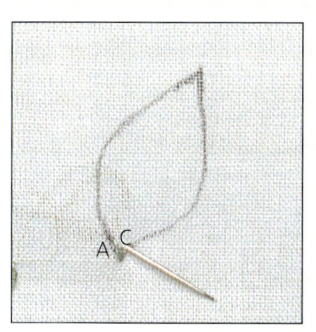

2. Pull the thread through. Re-emerge at C, on the opposite side to A.

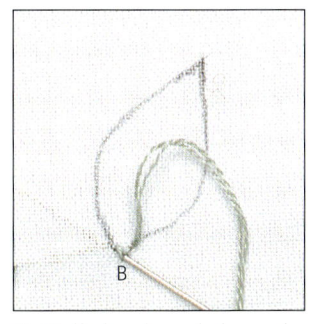

3. Pull the thread through. Take the needle to the back at B, using the same hole in the fabric as before.

4. Pull the thread through. Re-emerge at D, 1.5mm (1/16") away from A.

5. Pull the thread through. Take the needle to the back at A, using exactly the same hole in the fabric as before.

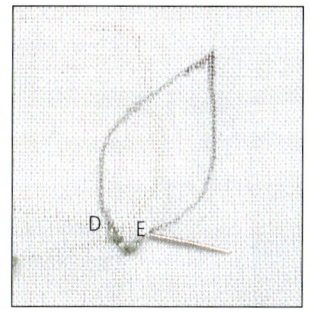

6. Pull the thread through and re-emerge at E, on the opposite side to D.

7. Pull the thread through. Take the needle to the back at C using the same hole in the fabric.

8. Continue working stitches following steps 4 - 7.

9. Continue until shape is filled. For last stitch, take needle to back and weave thread under stitches as close as possible to edge.

10. Right side of fabric. **Completed shadow work.**

40

ETERNITY

The sheer poetry of an opulent silk wedding cushion.

A worthy bearer of your most precious symbols of never ending love - your wedding rings.

Created by Carolyn Pearce of New South Wales

LOVERS ALONE WEAR SUNLIGHT
e.e. cummings

This stunning ring cushion showcases Carolyn's distinctive ribbon roses. A raised stem stitch band, signifying a lasting union, links clusters of voluptuous ribbon roses and pansies. Delicate orange blossom buds and forget-me-nots are sprinkled among the roses.

REQUIREMENTS

Fabric
110cm x 138cm wide (43" x 54 1/2") cream silk dupion
35cm x 80cm wide (13 3/4" x 31 1/2") piece of calico

Threads, Ribbons, Beads & Needles
See page 45.

Supplies
39cm (15 1/2") square of thin wadding (eg *Pellon*)
2.3m x 3mm wide (2yd 18 1/2" x 1/8") double-sided cream satin ribbon
4 x 13mm (1/2") mother-of-pearl buttons
Polyester fibre-fill
Natural *YLI* 70/2 ply heirloom sewing thread
White beading thread (eg *Nymo*)
Clear nylon thread
Quilting thread
Tracing paper
Sharp lead pencil
Black pen
12.5cm (5") embroidery hoop
30cm (12") embroidery hoop

PREPARATION FOR EMBROIDERY

See the liftout pattern for the cutting layout and embroidery design.

Cutting out
Cut a 39cm (15 1/2") square of silk dupion for the cushion front. This will be cut to the exact size after the embroidery is complete.

Transferring the design
Using the black pen, trace the embroidery design onto the tracing paper. Tape the tracing to a window or light box. With the right side facing up, centre the square of fabric over the tracing, aligning the straight grain of the fabric with the placement marks on the design. Tape in place.

Using the lead pencil, outline the sections of the band and the leaves. Mark the centres of the large roses and pansies with small circles. Mark the rosebuds, orange blossom buds and stems with lines and the forget-me-nots and remaining roses with small dots.

Backing the fabric
Pin the piece of thin wadding to the wrong side of the fabric. Using machine sewing thread, tack the two layers together in a grid pattern *(diag 1)*. Work a machine zigzag or overlock stitch around the edges to prevent fraying.

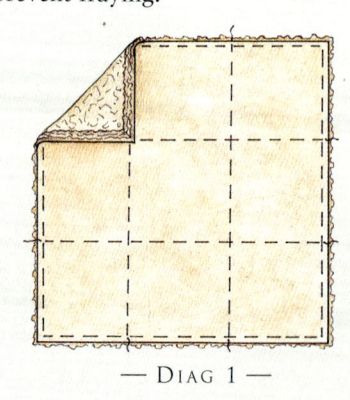

— DIAG 1 —

42

~ A CELEBRATION OF LOVE ~

EMBROIDERY

See pages 47 - 49 for step-by-step instructions for making a cabbage rose petal, small rose, ruched pansy and beaded forget-me-not.

Use the no. 18 chenille needle when stitching with the 7mm (5/16") ribbons and the no. 22 chenille needle when stitching with the 4mm (3/16") ribbons. Use the tapestry needle for working the raised stem stitch and the milliner's needle for rolling the cabbage rose petals and beading. The sharp needle is used when stitching with the heirloom sewing thread and the no. 8 crewel needle when stitching with six strands of thread. The no. 10 crewel needle is used for all other thread embroidery.

Order of work

Band

Each section is worked in a 12.5cm (5") embroidery hoop.

Work straight stitches approximately 2mm (1/16") apart to form the framework for the raised stem stitches. Work the bars to the outside of the pencil outline.

Starting at the same end each time, work rows of stem stitches across the framework, without going through the fabric. After each stitch pull the thread firmly, parallel with the bar. After every 2 - 3 rows, put your needle under the bars and push the rows down to pack them tightly together. The more rows you can fit in, the more raised and smooth the end result will be.

Cabbage roses

Make 10 - 12 petals for each rose following the instructions on page 48.

Embroider a very loose colonial knot for the centre of one rose. With the rolled edge facing outwards, attach the first inner petal very close to the centre. Take the thread through the roll at one end of the petal, dragging it under the colonial knot. Repeat for the other end of the petal. Attach two more petals in the same manner with each petal overlapping the previous one.

Secure four petals in the same manner for the middle round and then 3 - 5 petals for the outer round.

When all the petals are in place, manipulate them into the desired position and secure with tiny stab stitches.

Twirled ribbon roses

Thread the ribbon into the no. 18 chenille needle and bring it to the front of the fabric at the position for the centre of one rose. Holding the ribbon taut, twirl it in an anti-clockwise direction until it is tightly twisted. Hold the ribbon approximately 3cm (1 1/4") from the fabric and, still keeping it taut, fold the ribbon over to form a loop *(diag 2)*. Hold the two ends of the ribbon close to the fabric and release the loop. The ribbon will twist around itself forming a double coil. Hold the coil and take the needle to the back close to where it first emerged. Pull the ribbon through until the rose is the desired size. Secure with the heirloom sewing thread.

— DIAG 2 —

*"When cutting the variegated ribbon for the cabbage roses, I cut to take advantage of the colour variations. I make more petals than I need so that I have a good selection when forming the roses.
Use the darkest petals for the central round, the mid tone petals for the middle round and the lightest petals for the outer round."*

CAROLYN

*"You can achieve different effects with your cabbage roses by changing the way you stitch them to the fabric.
I have found that by stitching from the front to the back the petal will lie flat. However, if you want your rose to sit up more, stitch from the back to the front. Stitching both ways produces a rose with more character!"*

CAROLYN

THIS DESIGN USES

*Beading, Cabbage rose, Couching
Colonial knot, Detached chain
Fly stitch, Granitos, Raised stem stitch, Ribbon stitch, Ruching
Running stitch, Smocker's knot
Spider web rose, Straight stitch
Twirling, Twisted detached chain*

Using acid free tissue

Use acid free tissue to wrap the treasures you wish to store and place them in good cardboard boxes, preferably archival quality. These are usually available from museums that deal with textiles. Take care not to crush any raised embroidery and give each piece plenty of space. Never store fabrics in plastic as the moisture in natural fibres can result in mould or mildew.

Spider web roses

For each of the five roses, work five evenly spaced spokes with the heirloom sewing thread.

Using the no. 22 chenille needle, bring the ribbon to the front between two spokes, as close as possible to the centre. Working in an anti-clockwise direction, weave the ribbon over and under the spokes for one round. Pull firmly so the framework does not show at the centre. Weave a second round, loosening the tension slightly, and allowing the ribbon to twist. Continue weaving in this way until the spokes are entirely covered. Take the ribbon to the back and finish off securely.

Small roses

Work the small roses following the instructions on page 47.

Rosebuds

Begin each bud with a twisted detached chain for the middle petal. Add the side petals with ribbon stitch, starting slightly to one side at the base of the bud and crossing over to the opposite side. Work the ribbon stitch sepals in the same manner.

With the silk thread, work two straight stitches at the tip, a fly stitch around the bud and a straight stitch over the bud. Add a straight stitch for the stem and couch in place.

Orange blossom buds

The petals of each bud are formed with a granitos. Work five straight stitches side by side and then work a layer of four stitches over the top.

Using the green thread, work 2 - 3 straight stitches over each bud and two on each side. Embroider two straight stitches of different lengths beyond the tip of the bud. Add a granitos of 6 - 8 straight stitches directly below the base.

Stitch the stems in the same manner as the rosebud stems.

Ruched pansies

Work the pansies following the instructions on page 49.

Blue forget-me-nots

Embroider a colonial knot for the centre. Surround this with five colonial knots for the petals, stitching them in the order shown on the diagram *(diag 3)*.

Cream forget-me-nots

Stitch the cream forget-me-nots following the instructions on pages 47 - 48.

Leaves

Work the large fly stitch leaves in groups of two and three. Ensure each leaf in a group is worked with a different colour. Finish each leaf with a smocker's knot at the base.

Add pairs of small detached chains with long anchoring stitches to some of the forget-me-nots.

Butterfly

Attach the small glass butterfly to the top of the design with clear nylon thread.

Lovers' knot bow

Cut two 25cm (10") lengths of the satin ribbon and set them aside for tying the wedding rings onto the ribbon tails.

Starting 5cm (2") from one end, tie a series of knots in the remaining piece of ribbon at the intervals marked on the diagram *(diag 4)*.

Using a long length of quilting cotton, knot it and work a back stitch at A *(see diag 5)*. Pick up 2 - 3 threads of the ribbon between each knot until reaching B *(diag 5)*. Ensure the ribbon does not twist. Pull up the quilting thread tightly and back stitch at B to secure. Arrange the loops into a bow and take the needle through all the loops at the centre 2 - 3 times. Stitch the bow to the fabric. Work a beaded forget-me-not in the centre of the bow to hide the stitches.

Referring to the photograph, arrange the tails on the cushion so that each tail folds into a zigzag towards the lower corners. Pin at each fold with a fine lace pin. Starting near the bow and working towards the tails, couch the ribbon with colonial knots positioned near the folds.

Construction

See the liftout pattern.

Diag 5   B   A

Diag 4

5CM | 5CM APART | 10CM APART | 7.5CM APART | 5CM APART | 7.5CM APART | 10CM APART | 5CM APART | 5CM

THREADS, RIBBONS, BEADS & NEEDLES

Threads

DMC stranded cotton
A = 3774 buff

Kacoonda fine silk
B = 107 soft sage

YLI 601 fine metallic thread
C = 7 pale blue-green

Rajmahal Art silk
D = 311 Fresco oil

The Thread Gatherer Silk'n Colors stranded silk
E = 027 maidenhair fern

Soie Cristale by Caron
F = 1144 lemon

Waterlilies by Caron silk thread
G = 096 orange blossom

YLI silk floss
H = 181 gold-beige
I = 721 pale blue

Ribbons

Colour Streams hand dyed silk ribbon 4mm (3/16") wide
J = 4m (4yd 13 1/2") no. 18 antique ivory

Kacoonda hand dyed silk ribbon 4mm (3/16") wide
K = 2m (2yd 7") no. 107 soft sage

Toray Sillook ribbon yarn 4mm (3/16") wide
L = 50cm (20") no. 726 old gold

Colour Streams hand dyed silk ribbon 7mm (5/16") wide
M = 1m (40") no. 18 antique ivory

Kacoonda hand dyed silk ribbon 7mm (5/16") wide
N = 60cm (24") no. 6C dusky earth

Vintage Ribbons hand dyed silk ribbon 7mm (5/16") wide
O = 60cm (24") moonlight

YLI spark organdy 9mm (3/8") wide
P = 50cm (20") no. 56 soft beige

Colour Streams hand dyed silk ribbon 13mm (1/2") wide
Q = 2m (2yd 7") no. 18 antique ivory

Kacoonda hand dyed silk ribbon 13mm (1/2") wide
R = 50cm (20") no. 302 peace

Vintage Ribbons hand dyed silk ribbon 13mm (1/2") wide
S = 50cm (20") blush

Beads & Needles

Mill Hill glass seed beads
T = 00123 cream
U = 00557 gold

Mill Hill Glass Treasures
No. 12127 butterfly

No. 8 crewel needle
No. 10 crewel needle
No. 10 milliner's (straw) needle
No. 12 sharp needle
No. 18 chenille needle
No. 22 chenille needle
No. 26 tapestry needle

EMBROIDERY KEY

All thread embroidery is worked with one strand unless otherwise specified.

Band = F (raised stem stitch)

Large cabbage roses
Centre = N (colonial knot)
Petals = Q, R and S (cabbage rose petal)

Medium roses
= M (twirled ribbon rose), J (spider web rose)

Small roses = J (colonial knot - running stitch combination)

Rosebuds
Middle petal = J (twisted detached chain)
Side petals = J (ribbon stitch)

Sepals = K (ribbon stitch), B (fly stitch, straight stitch)
Stem = B (straight stitch, couching)
Tips = B (straight stitch)

Pansies
Petals = O and P (ruching)
Centre = L (colonial knot)

Orange blossom buds
Bud = G (2 strands, granitos)
Calyx = D (straight stitch, granitos)
Stem = D (straight stitch, couching)

Blue forget-me-nots
Centre = H (6 strands, colonial knot)
Petals = I (6 strands, colonial knot)

Cream forget-me-nots
Petals = T (beading)
Centre = U (beading)

Leaves
Large leaves = B, C and E (fly stitch)
Small leaves = B and E (detached chain)

Lovers' knot bow
Couching = A (2 strands, colonial knot)

45

"I JUST LOVED EMBROIDERING THIS CUSHION AND TRIED TO CHOOSE FLOWERS THAT SENT MESSAGES OF LOVE AND FIDELITY.
I DESIGNED THE CUSHION SO IT CAN BE USED AFTERWARDS AS A LOVELY MEMENTO OF THE WEDDING. HENCE, THE RINGS ARE TIED ONTO THE TAILS OF THE BOW AND THE RIBBON CAN BE EASILY REMOVED."
CAROLYN

ETERNITY

The tails of a lovers' knot bow secure the two gold rings. The cushion is finished with a generous frill and is neatly buttoned at the back with mother-of-pearl buttons. The finished cushion measures 43.5cm x 51cm wide (17 1/8" x 20 1/8").

Step-by-step small rose

A combination of running stitches and a colonial knot are used to create this ingenious rose.

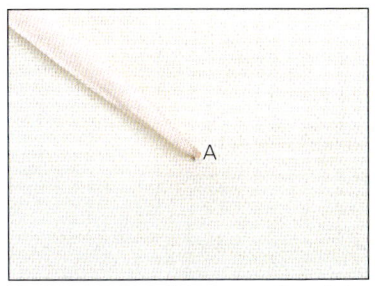

1. Bring the ribbon to the right side of the fabric at A.

2. Wrap the ribbon around the needle as if making a colonial knot, but approx 5 - 6cm (2-2 3/8") from the fabric.

3. Take 6 - 8 running stitches, each approx 6mm (1/4") long, down the middle of the ribbon. Keep the stitches the same length.

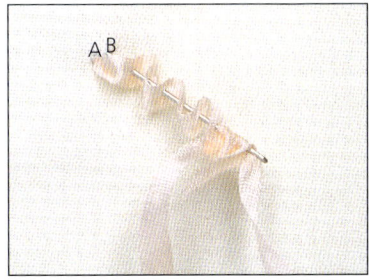

4. Insert the needle into the fabric at B, close to A. Ensure this last stitch is the same length as the previous stitches.

5. Tighten the knot around the needle. Begin to pull the needle through to the back of the fabric.

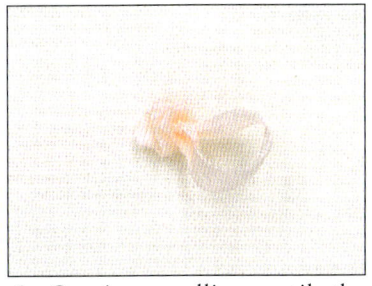

6. Continue pulling until the ribbon folds up into petals with a colonial knot in the middle.

7. End off on the back of the fabric. Adjust the petals with the eye of the needle. **Completed rose.**

Step-by-step beaded forget-me-not

1. Flower. Using a 30cm (12") length of beading thread and the milliner's needle, thread on six cream beads.

2. Pass the needle and thread through the first three beads to form a circle.

3. Thread on a gold bead. Take the needle and thread through the sixth cream bead.

4. Pull firmly so the centre bead sits in the middle, slightly higher than the circle of cream beads.

5. Tightly knot the two ends of thread. Finish off one tail and use remaining tail to couch circlet of beads to the fabric.

6. Leaves. Work a pair of detached chain leaves using long anchoring stitches. **Completed forget-me-not.**

STEP-BY-STEP CABBAGE ROSE PETAL

1. Cut a 26mm (1") length of ribbon. Work running stitches along left end and halfway along lower edge. Leave thread dangling.

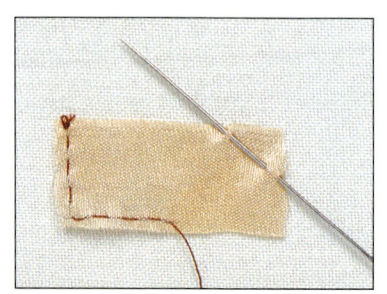

2. Pin the milliner's needle diagonally across the top right corner.

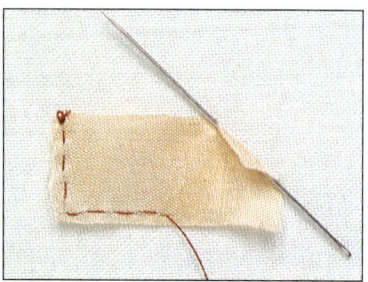

3. Fold the corner of the ribbon over the needle.

4. Roll the ribbon tightly until the needle lines up with both ends of the running stitch.

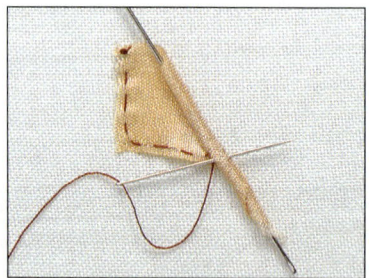

5. Pick up the dangling thread. Take a stitch through the roll.

6. Remove the milliner's needle. Pull up the running stitches so the petal cups slightly.

7. Secure the thread with two back stitches and cut off the excess.

8. Carefully trim tail of ribbon near back stitches. Trim any whiskers of ribbon or thread. **Completed petal.**

STEP-BY-STEP RUCHED PANSY

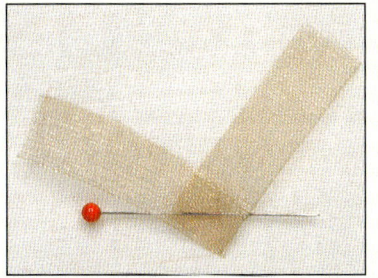

1. Upper petals. Cut two pieces of spark organdy, each 3cm (1 1/4") long. Place the two pieces at right angles, overlapping the ends. Pin.

2. Secure the thread at A. Work running stitches across the corners and along the edges as shown.

3. Pull up the running stitches so the stitches form a slight arc with a pointed tail at the centre. Back stitch to secure the thread.

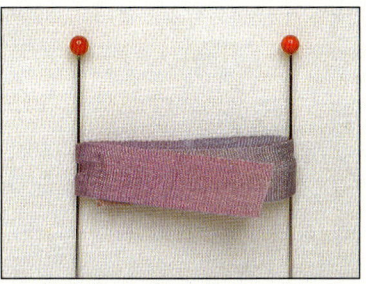

4. Middle and lower petals. Cut an 8.5cm (3 3/8") length of ribbon. Fold the ribbon into thirds and mark each fold with a pin.

5. Refold the ribbon as shown. Pin the diagonal folds.

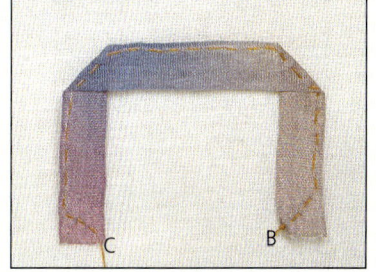

6. Secure the thread at B with a knot. Work running stitches across the corners and along the edges as shown until reaching C.

7. Pull up the running stitches tightly and back stitch to secure. Do not cut off the thread.

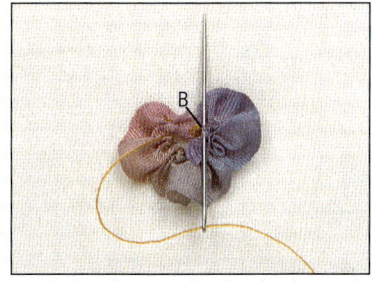

8. Take the needle back through the ribbon at B.

9. Pull the thread through to form a circle. Secure with a back stitch.

10. Using the same thread, attach these petals to the upper petals. Ensure the upper petals sit well above the middle petals.

11. Secure the pansy to the fabric with tiny stab stitches around the centre hole.

12. End off the thread. Using ribbon, work a colonial knot at the centre. **Completed ruched pansy.**

49

BELOVED

Elegance at its most breathtaking.

This timeless little stumpwork handbag will lend a romantic touch to your bridal gown or going away outfit.

Designed by Jane Nicholas
of New South Wales

51

THE INSPIRATION FOR THIS EXQUISITE STUMPWORK BAG CAME FROM THE VERY ELABORATE SWEET BAGS OF THE SIXTEENTH AND SEVENTEENTH CENTURIES. THESE ORIGINAL BAGS CONTAINED SCENTED HERBS AND ESSENCES TO SWEETEN THE AIR AND WERE OFTEN USED AS ELABORATE GIFT PACKAGING.

The front of the bag features a butterfly surrounded by a stylised vine. Thistles, foxgloves, carnation and heartsease bloom among the coiling stems. The finished bag, excluding the handle, measures 12cm (4 3/4") square.

REQUIREMENTS

Fabric

50cm x 85cm wide (19 3/4" x 29 1/2") piece of ivory silk dupion

40cm x 100cm wide (15 3/4" x 39 1/2") piece of quilter's muslin

40cm x 85cm wide (15 3/4" x 29 1/2") piece of white felt

Threads Beads & Needles

See page 55.

Supplies

40cm x 60cm wide (15 3/4" x 23 5/8") piece of paper-backed fusible web (eg *Vliesofix*)

1.5m (1yd 23") white fine flower wire

3cm x 11cm wide (1 1/8" x 4 3/8") piece of plastic canvas

30cm x 6mm wide (11 3/4" x 1/4") piping cord

Clear nylon thread

23cm (9") embroidery hoop

10cm (4") embroidery hoop

Tracing paper (eg *Gladbake*)

Sharp lead pencil

Eyebrow comb

Fine tweezers

CUTTING OUT

See the liftout pattern for the pattern and cutting layouts.

Bag front

Following the cutting layout, cut a 33cm (13") square of silk dupion for the bag front. Cut three more 33cm (13") squares, one each from the felt, quilter's muslin and fusible web.

Detached design pieces

Cut three pieces of quilter's muslin, each 20cm (8") square.

PREPARATION FOR EMBROIDERY

See the liftout pattern for the embroidery design and templates.

Bag front

Transferring the design

Trace the bag front pattern piece, including the embroidery design, onto tracing paper with the lead pencil.

Tape the square of muslin to a hard surface to prevent movement. Centre the tracing, right side down, over the muslin. Tape in place. Trace all the design lines and pattern markings with an empty ballpoint pen or a pencil. Remove the tracing.

HAPPILY EVER AFTER

THIS DESIGN USES

Back stitch, Beading, Blanket stitch, Bullion knot, Chain stitch, Couching, Detached chain
Fly stitch, French knot, Ghiordes knot, Lattice couching, Long and short stitch
Long and short blanket stitch, Needle weaving, Padded blanket stitch, Satin stitch, Split back stitch
Straight stitch, Van dyke stitch, Whipped chain stitch, Whipping

53

BELOVED

Preparing the fabrics

Fuse the square of felt to the wrong side of the square of silk dupion with the fusible web. Pin the fused fabrics to the muslin so the silk dupion and traced design are facing outwards. Tack the layers together around the edge and within the seam allowance of the bag front.

Mount the fabrics into the large embroidery hoop. Working from the back and using one strand of B, tack along the vines and leaf outlines with tiny stitches.

Detached design pieces

Using the lead pencil, trace the petals for the heartsease onto a piece of tracing paper. Trace the wings for the butterfly onto a second piece of tracing paper and the foxglove shapes onto a third piece.

Transfer each set of shapes to a square of quilter's muslin just before you are ready to embroider that section of the design. Each set of shapes is transferred following the procedure below.

Place the square of muslin in the small hoop ensuring it is 'drum' tight. Place a lid or similar object behind the fabric to give you a firm surface. Centre the tracing, right side down, over the muslin. Tape in place to prevent movement. Trace the shape outlines with an empty ballpoint pen or a pencil. Remove the tracing.

Felt padding

Cut a piece of felt, 4.5cm x 15cm wide (1 3/4" x 6"). Cut a piece of fusible web the same size.

Using the lead pencil, trace the carnation and thistle padding pieces onto the paper side of the fusible web. Label each piece inside the outline. Fuse the tracing to the felt. Carefully cut out each shape.

EMBROIDERY

See pages 56 - 61 for step-by-step instructions for couching with van dyke stitch and for working the thistle, carnation, foxglove, heartsease and butterfly.

Use the no. 10 crewel needle when stitching with one strand of thread, the no. 5 crewel needle when stitching with 2 - 3 strands of thread and the chenille needle when stitching with 6 - 7 strands of thread or the no. 5 perlé cotton.

The tapestry needle is used for the needle weaving, the yarn darner for sinking the wires and working with the chenille thread and the sharp needle for attaching the beads and sequins. The milliner's needle is used for stitching the ghiordes knots and working with the metallic thread.

Use the design lines on the muslin as references for positioning the stumpwork motifs and sequins.

Order of work

Vines and leaves

Bring the perlé cotton to the front at the tip of one vine near the centre top of the design. Lay it along the first section of the vine. Following the instructions on page 56 and using two strands of B, work van dyke stitch over the laid thread until reaching the second tendril. Change to three strands of B and continue to the base of the vine. Ensure the laid thread is kept taut while couching it in place. Using two strands of thread and beginning at the tip, couch the lower vine for approximately 4.5cm (1 3/4"). Change to three strands and complete the vine. Embroider the vines in the other half of the design in the same manner. Add the tendrils in whipped chain stitch.

Stitch the vein of one leaf in chain stitch. Outline the leaf shape in back stitch and fill with straight stitches for padding. Covering the back stitch outline, work blanket stitches from the edge to the centre vein along one half of the leaf. Repeat for the remaining half. Work the stem in whipped chain stitch. Embroider the remaining leaves in the same manner.

Foxgloves

First, embroider the stems in chain stitch. Stitch both foxgloves following the instructions on page 57.

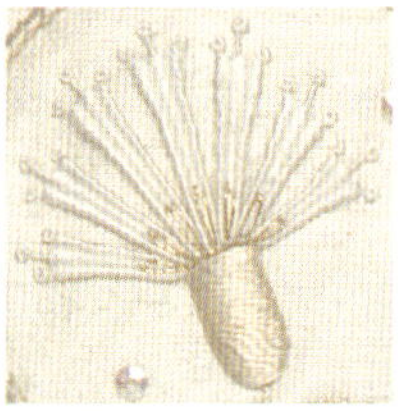

Carnation

Embroider the carnation following the instructions on page 58. Add the stem in chain stitch.

Thistles

Stitch the thistle following the instructions on page 59. Embroider the thistle bud in the same manner, using only two layers of padding for the base and trimming the ghiordes knots for the head to approximately 4mm (3/16"). Add the stems in chain stitch.

Heartsease

Following the instructions on page 60, create the five petals on the quilter's muslin. Cut out the petals and attach them to the bag front. Finish the flower with a French knot centre and chain stitch stem.

Butterfly

Embroider the wings and assemble the butterfly following the instructions on page 61.

Scattered sequins

Using the clear nylon thread, attach the cup sequins upside down at the positions indicated on the muslin backing.

CONSTRUCTION

See the liftout pattern.

THREADS, BEADS & NEEDLES

Au Ver à Soie, Soie d'Alger stranded silk
A = brut
B = F1 dk ivory
C = F2 ivory

DMC stranded cotton
D = blanc

Madeira stranded silk
E = 2401 soft white

Rajmahal Art silk
F = ecru
G = 96 white

DMC no. 5 perlé cotton
H = ecru

Au Ver à Soie, Soie Chenille à Broder
I = crème

Madeira no. 40 metallic thread
J = 3 gold

Beads
Mill Hill petite glass beads
K = 42027 champagne
22 x 3mm (1/8") cup sequins
L = crystal

Needles
No. 5 crewel needle
No. 10 crewel needle 
No. 9 milliner's (straw) needle
No. 12 sharp needle
No. 14 yarn darner
No. 18 chenille needle
No. 26 tapestry needle

EMBROIDERY KEY

All embroidery is worked with one strand of thread unless otherwise specified.

Vines and leaves

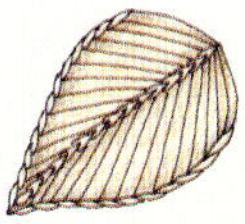

Vine = H (laid thread), B (2 - 3 strands, van dyke stitch)

Tendrils = B (2 strands, whipped chain stitch)

Leaf veins = E (chain stitch)

Leaf = C (back stitch, padded blanket stitch)

Leaf stems = C (whipped chain stitch)

Thistles

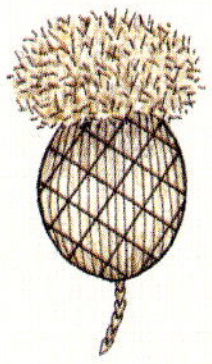

Base = B (blanket stitch, satin stitch)

Base markings = J (lattice couching)

Head = B blended with D, and B blended with E (1 strand of each, ghiordes knot)

Stems = B (2 strands, chain stitch)

Carnation

Calyx = B (blanket stitch, satin stitch)

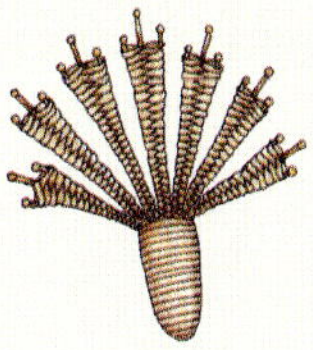

Petals = E (2 strands, needle weaving, whipping, French knot, 1 wrap)

Petal markings = J (detached chain)

Stem = B (2 strands, chain stitch)

Foxgloves

Lower edge = A (back stitch, blanket stitch)

Lip = A (couching, blanket stitch, split back stitch)

Trumpet = A (long and short blanket stitch, long and short stitch)

Sepals = J (detached chain)

Stamens = K (beading)

Stems = B (2 strands, chain stitch)

Heartsease

Upper petals = C (couching, blanket stitch, long and short blanket stitch), E (straight stitch)

Middle petals = E (couching, blanket stitch, long and short blanket stitch, straight stitch)

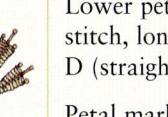

Lower petal = E (couching, blanket stitch, long and short blanket stitch), D (straight stitch)

Petal markings = J (straight stitch)

Centre = B (6 strands, French knot, 1 wrap)

Stem = B (2 strands, chain stitch)

Butterfly

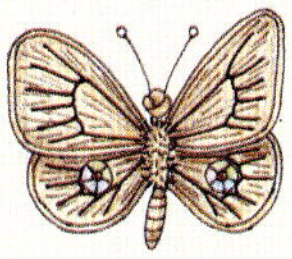

Wings = F (couching, blanket stitch, long and short blanket stitch), G (straight stitch)

Wing veins = J (fly stitch, blanket stitch)

Spots on front wings = B (French knot, 1 wrap)

Spots on back wings = B (French knot, 1 wrap), L (beading)

Head = A (7 strands, French knot, 1 wrap)

Thorax = I (straight stitch)

Abdomen = A (7 strands, bullion knot, 5 wraps)

Antennae = J (detached chain)

Scattered sequins = L (beading)

...I WAS AT A PARTY FEELING VERY SHY BECAUSE THERE WERE A LOT OF CELEBRITIES AROUND, AND I WAS SITTING IN A CORNER ALONE AND A VERY BEAUTIFUL YOUNG MAN CAME UP TO ME AND OFFERED ME SOME SALTED PEANUTS AND HE SAID, "I WISH THEY WERE EMERALDS" AS HE HANDED ME THE PEANUTS AND THAT WAS THE END OF MY HEART. I NEVER GOT IT BACK.

HELEN HAYES ON FIRST MEETING HER HUSBAND, CHARLES MACARTHUR

STEP-BY-STEP COUCHING WITH VAN DYKE STITCH

To achieve a raised braid effect, keep the stitches close together.

1. Bring laid thread to front at A. Lay it along marked line. Bring couching thread to front at B, just to left and below A.

2. Take the needle to the back at C, just to the right of A.

3. Pull the thread through. Re-emerge at D, just to the left of A.

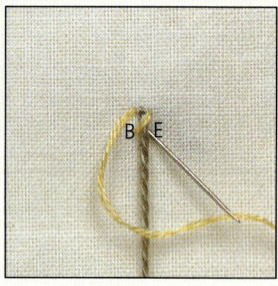

4. Pull the thread through. Take the needle to the back at E, directly opposite B.

5. Pull the thread through. Re-emerge at F, below B.

6. Pull the thread through. Slide the needle from right to left behind the laid thread and the crossed threads.

7. Pull the thread through. Take the needle to the back at G.

8. Pull thread through. Re-emerge at H. Take the needle behind the laid thread and the last set of crossed threads.

9. Pull thread through. Continue in the same manner until near the end of the laid thread.

10. Take the laid thread to the back of the fabric at the end of the design line.

11. Continue working stitches to the end of laid thread. Take needle to back of fabric just to the right of laid thread.

12. End off both threads on the back of the fabric. **Completed couching with van dyke stitch.**

STEP-BY-STEP STUMPWORK FOXGLOVE

The detached section of the foxglove is embroidered onto quilter's muslin before attaching it to the background fabric.

1. Lower section. On the main fabric, outline the foxglove shape in back stitch. Work the stem in chain stitch.

2. Work blanket stitches along the lower edge, covering approximately one third of the shape.

3. Detached section. Cut a 4cm (1 1/2") length of wire. Centre it across lower edge of shape. Couch in place, leaving ends free.

4. Work blanket stitch over the wire for the width of the lower edge.

5. Outline the shape in split back stitch. Work a row of long and short blanket stitch close to the wire.

6. Fill the remainder of the shape with long and short stitch.

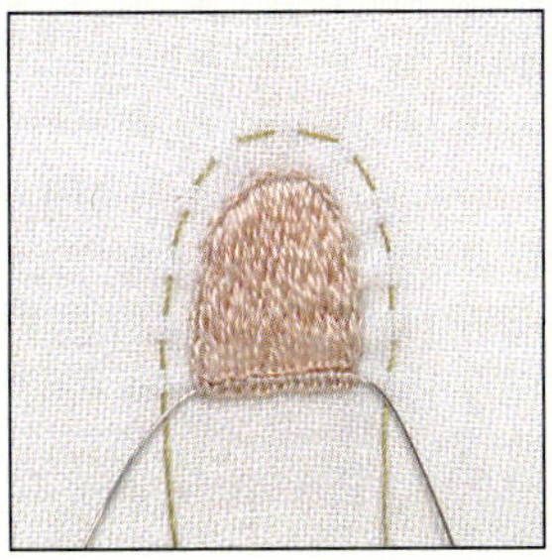

7. Work running stitch along sides and top 1.5mm (1/16") from edge. Leave a 5cm (2") tail of thread at each end.

8. Carefully cut out the shape approx 3mm (1/8") out from running stitches. Cut as close as possible to wire on lower edge.

9. Attaching the detached section. Gently pull the thread tails to ease the seam allowance to the inside.

10. Secure the top to the end of the stem with a stab stitch. Sink the wires at the lower corners of the trumpet.

11. Twist the wires together on the back and secure behind the embroidery. Trim excess wire.

Wrong side of fabric

12. Gently pulling the thread tails to ease the shape to size, secure sides and top of shape to fabric with stab stitches.

13. Trim the thread tails. Insert a tiny amount of fibrefill into flower. Push in with a skewer or similar object.

14. Starting at stem, stitch five detached chains over top of flower. Secure three beads for stamens. **Completed foxglove.**

57

WEDDING FOLKLORE

The shape of the modern three tiered iced cake is believed to have been inspired by the spire of Saint Bride's Church in London. It is said that unmarried guests who place a piece of wedding cake under their pillow before sleeping will increase their prospects of finding a partner and bridesmaids who do likewise will dream of their future husbands.

Step-by-step stumpwork carnation

1. Padding. Using stab stitches, attach the sides and lower edge of the felt padding to the fabric.

2. Stitch around the sides and lower edge in blanket stitch.

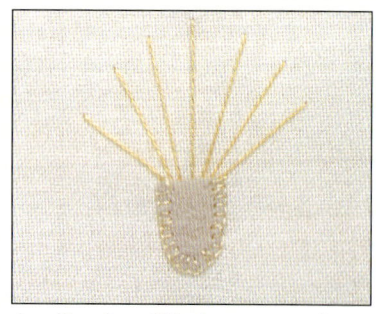

3. Petals. Work seven long straight stitches from just under the top of the felt to the marked dots on the back of the fabric.

4. Work a slightly shorter straight stitch on each side of each long straight stitch. Ensure the stitches are well secured.

5. Using a 25cm (10") long thread, work needleweaving from base to tip of one petal. Relax tension as you work towards top.

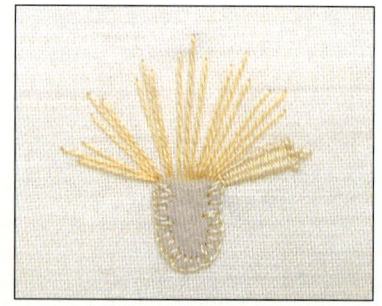

6. Using same thread, whip the remainder of the middle straight stitch. Work a French knot at the tip of each straight stitch.

7. Work the remaining six petals in the same manner.

8. Beginning on the felt each time, work a detached chain onto the base of each petal.

9. Calyx. Completely cover the felt padding and ends of the petals with horizontal satin stitches. **Completed carnation.**

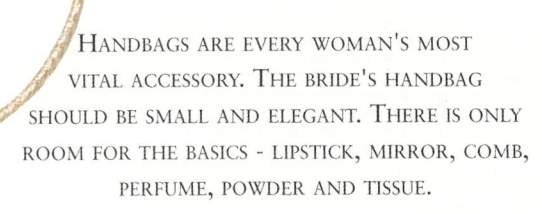

Handbags are every woman's most vital accessory. The bride's handbag should be small and elegant. There is only room for the basics - lipstick, mirror, comb, perfume, powder and tissue.

Step-by-Step Stumpwork Thistle

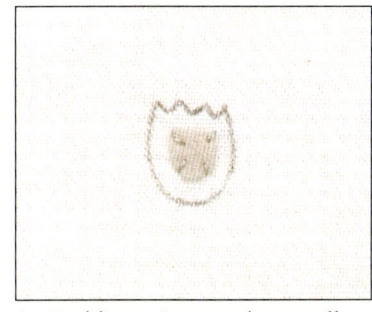

1. Padding. Secure the smallest piece of felt to the centre of the marked outline with stab stitches.

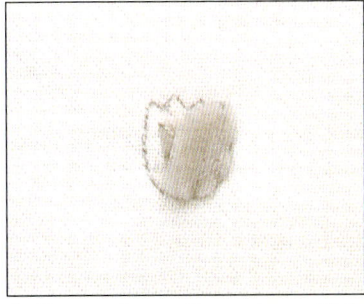

2. Centre the medium piece of felt over the first and attach with stab stitches. Repeat for the largest piece of felt.

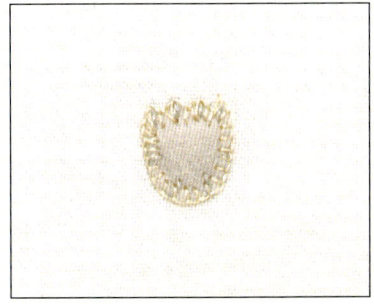

3. Stitch around all sides in blanket stitch.

4. Base. Starting at the centre, cover half of the felt with satin stitches.

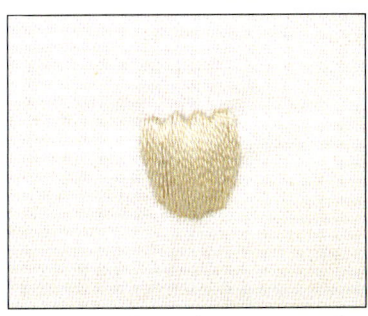

5. Starting from the centre again, cover the remaining half of the felt in the same manner.

6. Cover base with long diagonal straight stitches. Work all stitches in one direction before working those in the opposite direction.

7. Couch each intersection with a tiny vertical straight stitch. Take the stitches right through to the back of the fabric.

8. Head. Starting in the 'valleys' between tips of the base, work a row of ghiordes knots. Hold the loops of thread out of the way.

9. Continue working rows of knots close together until head is covered. Alternate between the two thread colour combinations.

10. Cut loops of knots to approx 1cm (3/8") and comb. Continue combing and trimming until head is desired shape. **Completed thistle.**

STEP-BY-STEP STUMPWORK HEARTSEASE

The detached petals are embroidered onto quilter's muslin before attaching them to the background fabric.

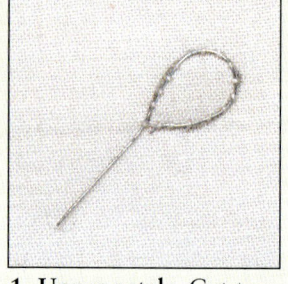

1. Upper petals. Cut two pieces of wire, each 8cm (3") long. Starting at base, couch one piece of wire to one petal shape.

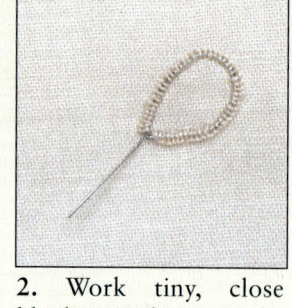

2. Work tiny, close blanket stitches over the wire, incorporating the couching stitches.

3. Cover upper 1/3 of petal with long and short blanket stitches worked close to inside edge of wire.

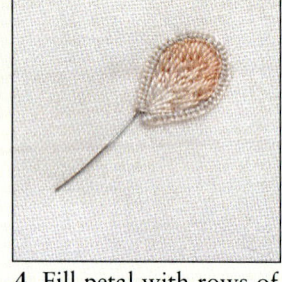

4. Fill petal with rows of straight stitches angled towards flower centre. Work second petal in same manner.

5. Middle petals. Cut two 8cm (3") pieces of wire. Work petals as for upper petals. Add three straight stitches for petal markings.

6. Lower petal. Cut an 8cm (3") length of wire. Leaving a tail of wire on each side, work petal in same manner as before.

7. Add seven radiating straight stitches of varying lengths for the petal markings.

8. Leaving the tails of wire intact, cut out each petal as close as possible to the stitching.

9. Attaching the petals. At marked position on background fabric, sink wire of one upper petal with the yarn darner.

10. Secure the tail of wire on the back with small stitches.

11. Attach remaining upper petal, middle petals, then lower petal. Secure each wire before sinking next one. Trim wires.

12. Centre. Work a loose French knot for the centre.

13. Shaping. Using the tweezers, carefully shape the petals. **Completed heartsease.**

Step-by-step Stumpwork Butterfly

The detached wings are embroidered onto quilter's muslin before attaching them to the background fabric.

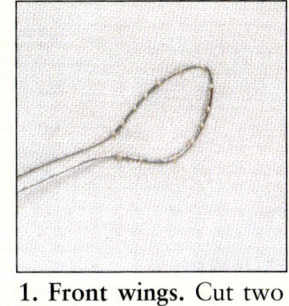

1. Front wings. Cut two 8cm (3") pieces of wire. Leave a tail of wire at each end and start at base. Couch one wire to wing shape.

2. Work tiny, close blanket stitches over the wire, incorporating the couching stitches.

3. Along the outer edge, work a row of long and short blanket stitch just inside the wire. Angle stitches towards base.

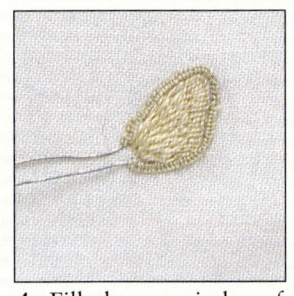

4. Fill the remainder of the wing with rows of straight stitch. Blend the rows into each other.

5. Beginning with a fly stitch and then working blanket stitches, embroider the wing veins.

6. Stitch a French knot in each wing section for the spots. Make the remaining upper wing in the same manner as the first.

7. Back wings. Make back wings in the same manner as front wings. Secure a sequin to each wing before working veins and spots.

8. Assembling wings. Cut out each wing as close as possible to the stitching but do not cut the wires.

9. Sink wires of one back wing through 2nd and 3rd marked dots on fabric. Repeat for 2nd wing. Fix wires on back and trim.

10. Sink the wires of one front wing through 1st and 2nd dots. Repeat for remaining front wing. Secure wires as before.

11. Body. With the chenille thread, work a straight stitch over the wing join for the thorax.

12. Stitch a French knot at upper end of thorax for the head. Stitch a bullion knot at the other end for the abdomen.

13. Antennae. Work two tiny detached chains with very long anchoring stitches.

14. Shaping. Carefully shape the wings with fine tweezers. **Completed butterfly.**

61

BLISS

It's the finer details that transform the ordinary into the extraordinary.

This exquisite mirror is designed to slip into your wedding bag.

Designed by Jane Nicholas
of New South Wales

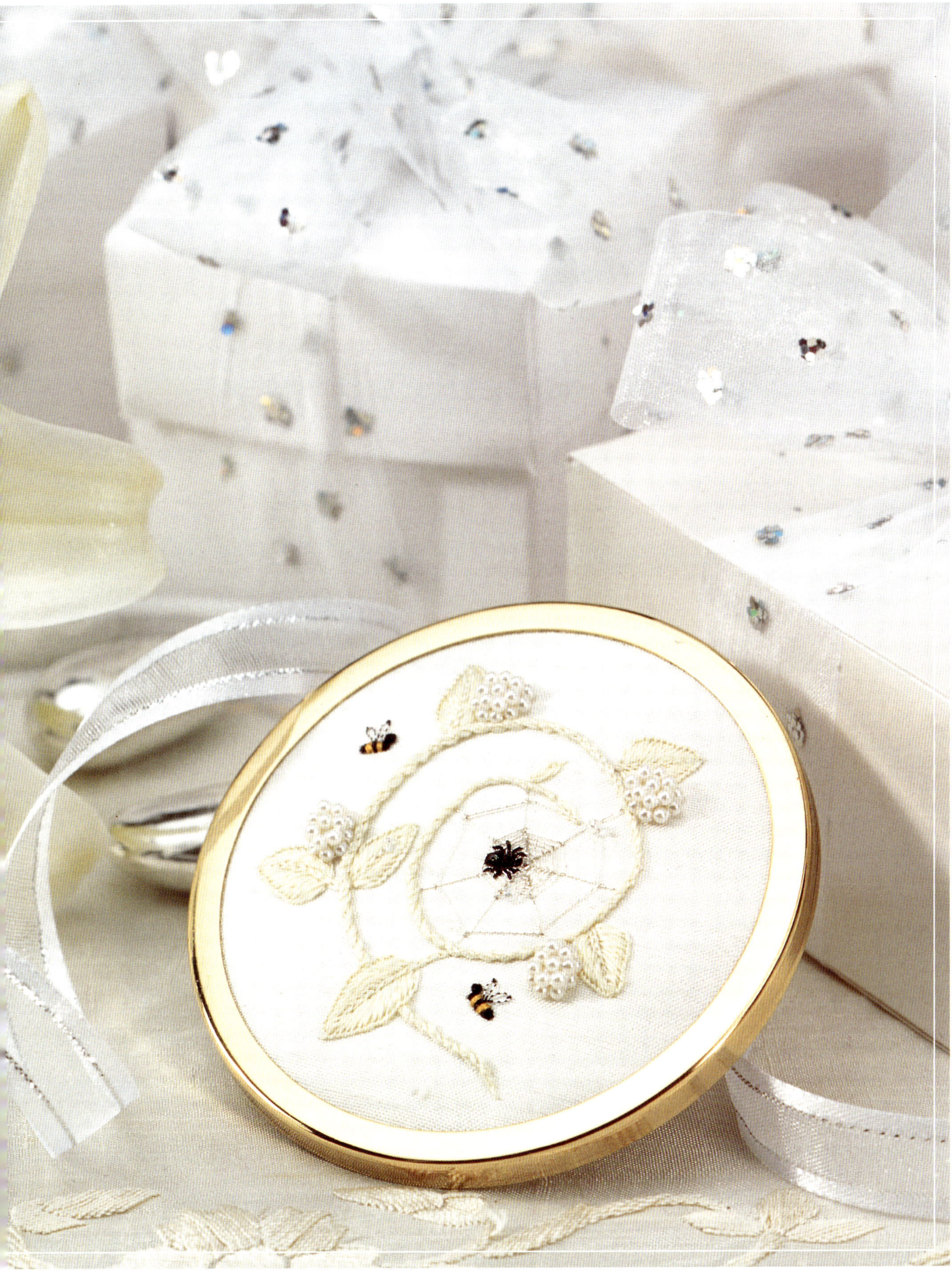

LOVE IS A CANVAS FURNISHED BY NATURE AND EMBROIDERED BY IMAGINATION. *ANONYMOUS*

BLISS

*A vine of beaded berries encloses a spider
and web on the back of this circular handbag mirror.
Two tiny bees hover among the foliage to complete the design.
The finished mirror measures 6.75cm (2 5/8") in diameter.*

REQUIREMENTS

Fabric
20cm (8") square of silk dupion

20cm (8") square of quilter's muslin

Threads, Beads & Needles
See opposite page.

Supplies
60mm (2 3/8") *Framecraft* handbag mirror

10cm (4") embroidery hoop

Tracing paper

Sharp lead pencil

PREPARATION FOR EMBROIDERY

See the liftout pattern for the embroidery design.

Transferring the design
Using the lead pencil, trace the embroidery design onto the tracing paper.

Centre the tracing face down on the right side of the silk dupion. Ensure the placement marks on the tracing are aligned with the straight grain of the fabric. Pin in place to prevent movement. Pressing firmly, retrace the design lines. Remove the tracing.

Preparing the fabric
With the right side uppermost, place the silk dupion over the quilter's muslin. Mount both fabrics in the hoop, stretching them 'drum' tight.

EMBROIDERY

See page 67 for step-by-step instructions for working a beaded berry.

Use the milliner's needle for attaching the dewdrops and when stitching with the metallic thread. Use the sharp needle for working the beaded berries and the no. 10 crewel needle when stitching with one strand of thread. The no. 8 crewel needle is used for all other embroidery.

Order of work

Vine
Leaving a space for the first leaf that overlaps the vine, and using three strands of thread, work chain stitch from the base of the vine to the fourth large leaf.

Remove one strand from the needle. Thread it onto a spare needle and take it to the back. End off the thread by working 2 - 3 tiny back stitches through the previous stitching. Using the remaining two strands of thread, continue working the vine in chain stitch until approximately 1.5cm (5/8") from the end. Remove another strand from the needle and end off as before. Embroider the last section of the vine using the remaining strand of thread.

Whip back along the entire vine with one strand of thread. When reaching the end, work a single detached chain.

Large leaves
Using one strand of thread, work the stems and centre veins of the leaves in chain stitch.

Pad the leaf shapes by filling with straight stitches. Beginning at the base, work very close blanket stitches over the padding on one side of a leaf. Repeat on the second side. Work the remaining leaves in the same manner. Attach a crystal bead to one leaf for a dewdrop.

Small leaves
Stitch two small leaves near the tip of the vine. For each leaf, work two detached chains, one inside the other.

~ WEDDED BLISS ~

Bees
Stitch a granitos of seven stitches to create the body padding. Work two satin stitches in black thread across the middle of the body. Using the topaz thread, stitch two satin stitches on each side of the black stripe. With the black thread, work two more satin stitches at each end. Embroider a French knot just above one end for the head. Add two detached chains to the top of the body for wings.

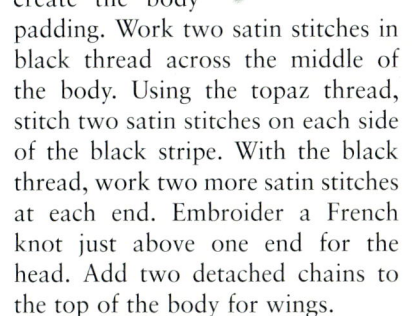

"I use two needles, one for the black thread and one for the topaz."
JANE

Spider web
Work seven long straight stitches to form the framework for the web. Take each stitch from the vine to the dot marked on the fabric.

Beginning at the centre and spiralling the rounds of stitches outwards, work a back stitch over each spoke. Keep the rounds close together. Form a tiny dewdrop by threading a crystal bead onto the needle between two back stitches in the last close round.

Work a row of back stitches in the same manner near the ends of the spokes. Add a second crystal bead to this row.

Spider
Work two tiny granitos next to each other to form the spider's thorax and abdomen. Add two French knots to the tip of the thorax for eyes.

Beginning at the thorax, work the eight legs. Each leg is 2 - 3 minute back stitches.

Using the blending filament, work the stripe on the abdomen with two straight stitches.

Berries
Work four berries following the instructions on page 67.

CONSTRUCTION
See the liftout pattern.

THREADS, BEADS & NEEDLES

DMC stranded cotton	*Cifonda Art silk*
A = 310 black	G = black
B = 783 med topaz	*Machine silk stitch 50*
Au Ver à Soie, Soie d'Alger stranded silk	H = white
C = 2131 ultra lt olive green	*Pearl beads 1.5mm ($1/16$") wide*
Madeira no. 40 metallic thread	I = cream
D = silver	*Mill Hill petite glass beads*
Kreinik metallic cord	J = 40161 crystal
E = 105C silver-black	No. 8 crewel needle
Kreinik metallic blending filament	No. 10 crewel needle
F = 085 peacock	No. 9 milliner's (straw) needle
	No. 12 sharp needle

EMBROIDERY KEY

All embroidery is worked with one strand of thread unless otherwise specified.

Vine
Main stem = C (1 - 3 strands, chain stitch; 1 strand, whipping, detached chain)
Large leaves = C (chain stitch, straight stitch, blanket stitch)
Dewdrop = J (beading)
Small leaves = C (detached chain)
Berries = H and I (beading)

Web = D (straight stitch, back stitch), J (beading)
Spider
Body = G (granitos)
Body stripe = F (straight stitch)
Eyes = G (French knot, 1 wrap)
Legs = G (back stitch)
Bees
Body = A and B (padded satin stitch)
Head = A (French knot, 2 wraps)
Wings = E (detached chain)

Wedding Folklore

The fortune of a spider

IF THE BRIDE IS WAKENED ON HER WEDDING MORN BY THE SONG OF A BIRD,
EVEN THOUGH IT IS ONLY THE CHIRPING OF A SPARROW, SHE MAY ACCEPT THAT AS A GOOD AUGURY;
ALSO, IF SHE DISCOVERS A SPIDER IN THE FOLDS OF HER DRESS - AN UNLIKELY THING,
UNLESS PUT THERE BY THE KIND AGENCY OF A FRIEND - THE RESULTS WILL BE ALL TO THE GOOD.

THIS DESIGN USES

*Back stitch, Beading, Blanket stitch, Chain stitch, Detached chain, French knot, Granitos
Padded satin stitch, Straight stitch, Whipped chain stitch*

STEP-BY-STEP BEADED BERRIES

The beads are applied individually with back stitches.
Each berry is formed from two layers of beads to give a three dimensional appearance.

1. First layer. Anchor thread on back. Work a straight stitch 3mm (1/8") long along centre mark. Bring thread to front near middle of straight stitch.

2. Thread a bead onto needle and slide down to the fabric. Take a stitch under the bead, re-emerging at the other end of the straight stitch.

3. Pull thread through. Thread a second bead onto the needle and slide down to the fabric. Take needle to back at beginning of previous stitch.

4. Pull thread through. Re-emerge on the right hand side of the centre beads. Attach a third bead with a back stitch.

5. Stitching in an anti-clockwise direction, attach eight more beads in the same manner to form a ring around the two centre beads.

6. Take the thread through each bead in the ring. Pull the thread firmly to draw the beads into a tight oval. Repeat twice.

7. Second layer. Take the needle to the back and re-emerge between the centre beads.

8. Pull the thread through. Thread a bead onto the needle. Take the needle to the back between the centre beads.

9. Bring the needle to the front just inside the oval of beads.

10. Attach seven beads in a circle around the centre bead. Stab needle up and down between the lower beads to work the back stitches.

11. Bring thread to front. Run the thread through the circle of beads three times. After each round, pull firmly to draw beads into a tight circle.

12. Take the thread to the back between the beads and end off. **Completed beaded berry.**

67

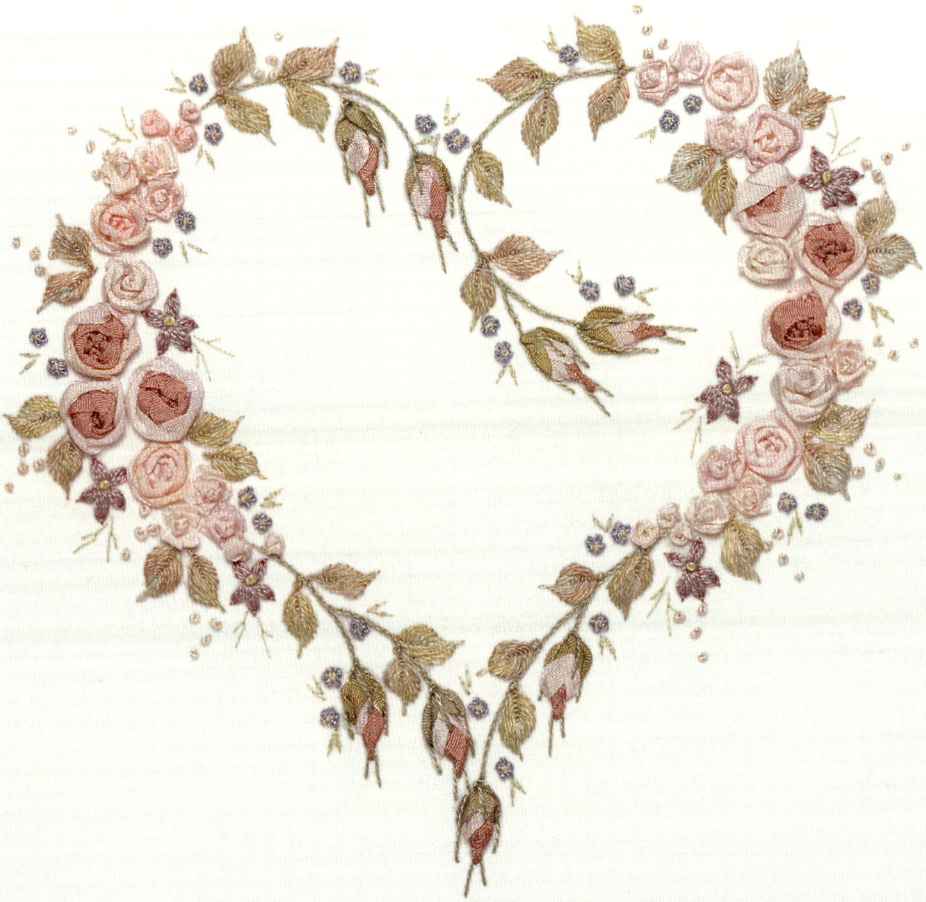

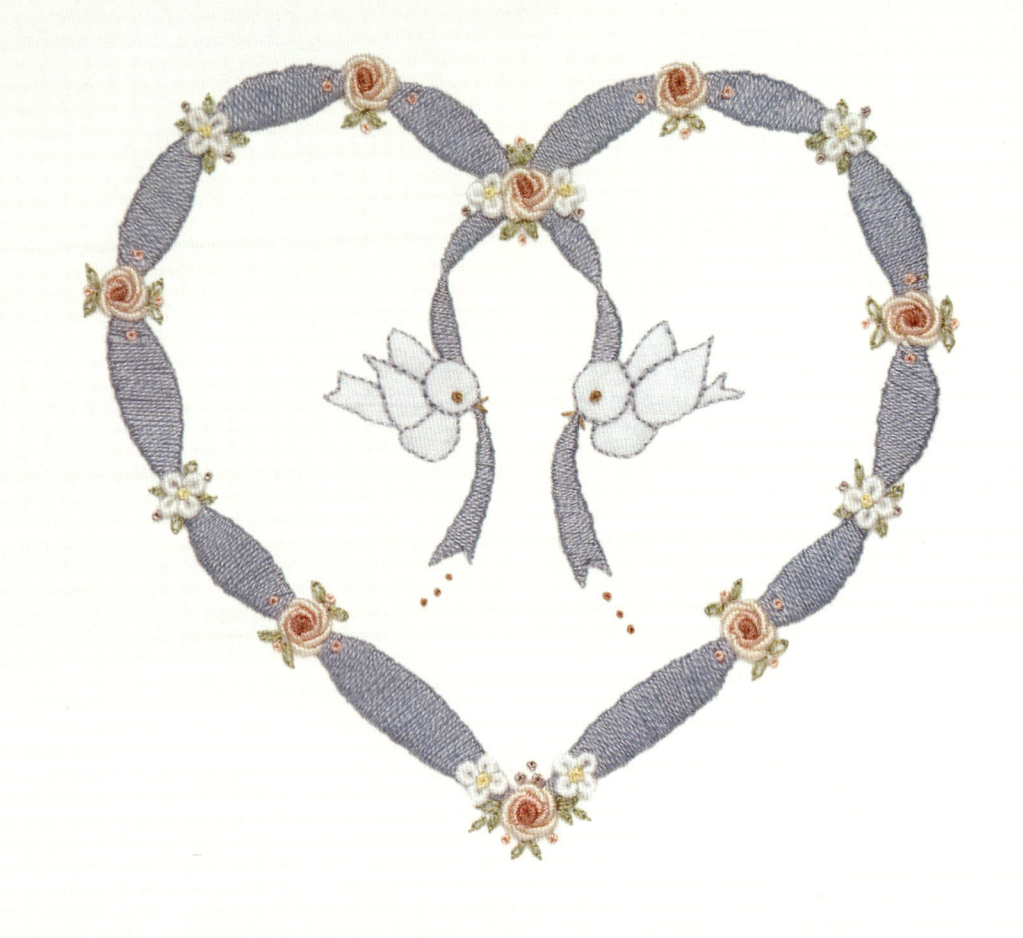

Designs of the Heart

A series of endearing designs perfect for your trousseau

~ DESIGNS OF THE HEART ~

TRANSFERRING THE DESIGNS

As these designs are intended for use on a wide variety of fabrics, we offer you three methods for transferring them. Choose the one that is most suitable for your fabric.

Lightweight, semi-translucent fabrics

Trace the design onto tracing paper using a black pen. With the right side of the fabric facing you, place it over the tracing. Align the placement marks on the design with the straight grain of the fabric. Pin in place to prevent movement. Using a sharp lead pencil, trace the design.

Medium weight fabrics

Trace the design onto the tracing paper using a black pen. Tape the tracing to a light box or window. With the right side of the fabric facing you, place it over the tracing, aligning the straight grain of the fabric with the placement marks on the design. Tape in place. Using a sharp lead pencil, trace the design.

Heavy weight or opaque fabrics

Trace the design onto tissue paper using a sharp lead pencil. Position the tracing onto the right side of the fabric, aligning the placement marks on the design with the straight grain of the fabric. Using contrasting machine sewing thread and small tacking stitches, tack the design to the fabric. Tack along the main design lines and mark the centres of large flowers with small crosses. Lightly moisten the tissue paper with a damp sponge, wait a few seconds, then carefully remove the paper. Alternatively, score along the tacking stitches with a needle. Carefully tear away the tissue paper, leaving the tacking stitches in place.

Most tacking threads marking the design can remain in the work permanently as the embroidery will cover them.

~ Ribbon Rose Heart ~

BY CAROLYN PEARCE OF NEW SOUTH WALES

Divine ribbon roses in a multitude of gentle hues decorate this elegant heart. Tiny forget-me-nots and dainty violets nestle among the leaves.

REQUIREMENTS

Threads, Ribbons & Needles

See opposite page.

Supplies

15cm (6") embroidery hoop

PREPARATION FOR EMBROIDERY

See the liftout pattern for the embroidery design and this page for instructions for transferring the design.

EMBROIDERY

See page 76 for step-by-step instructions for the dark stem stitch rose and ribbon rosebud, and page 47 for the small rose.

Refer to the design in the centre liftout for the placement of each type of rose.

Order of work

Dark stem stitch roses

Work these roses first, following the instructions on page 76. Use the no. 22 chenille needle when working the colonial knots and the no. 18 chenille needle for the stem stitch.

Light stem stitch roses

Using the no. 18 chenille needle and the antique rose ribbon, embroider three stem stitch roses. Start at the outer edge of the rose and work stem stitch in a spiral towards the middle. Finish with a loose colonial knot at the centre.

Spider web roses

For each of the five roses, work five evenly spaced spokes with thread. Using the no. 22 chenille needle, bring the ribbon to the front between two spokes as close as possible to the centre. Working in an anti-clockwise direction, weave the ribbon over and under the spokes for one round. Pull firmly so the framework does not show at the centre. Weave a second round, loosening the tension slightly, and allowing the ribbon to twist. Continue weaving in this way until the spokes are entirely covered.

Small roses

Work the small roses following the instructions on page 47.

Clusters of ribbon knots

Embroider three clusters of ribbon knots using the no. 18 chenille needle. Stitch the clusters in the upper left and lower right sections of the design using two French knots and one colonial knot. Work a French knot and a colonial knot in the lower left section.

Rosebuds

Work the rosebuds following the instructions on page 76. Use the no. 22 chenille needle when stitching with the ribbon and the no. 10 crewel needle when stitching with the thread.

Stems

Using the no. 8 crewel needle, work the stems in stem stitch.

Violets

Embroider a granitos of five straight stitches for each of the five petals. Make the stitches approximately 4mm (3/16") long and use the no. 10 crewel needle. Work the petals in the order shown on the diagram *(diag 1)*.

DIAG 1

Using the mauve thread, add a fly stitch around the tip of each petal and a straight stitch over each tip.

Large leaves

Embroider the fly stitch leaves using the no. 10 crewel needle. Finish each leaf with a smocker's knot at the base.

Forget-me-nots

Using the no. 8 crewel needle, embroider a colonial knot for the centre of each flower. Surround this with five colonial knots for the petals, stitching them in the order shown on the diagram *(diag 2)*.

DIAG 2

Small leaves

Embroider pairs of small fly stitch leaves near the violets and detached chain leaves near the forget-me-nots.

Sprays of small knots

Stitch the knots with the no. 8 crewel needle. Embroider three colonial knots in a triangle and finish with a French knot at the tip.

THIS DESIGN USES

Colonial knot
Colonial knot-running stitch combination
Detached chain, Fly stitch, French knot
Granitos, Ribbon stitch, Smocker's knot
Spider web rose, Stem stitch
Straight stitch, Twisted detached chain

THREADS, RIBBONS & NEEDLES

Madeira stranded silk

A = 0807 lt antique violet

B = 0901 lt blue-violet

C = 1510 lt green-grey

D = 1910 lt mushroom

E = 2207 vy lt old gold

YLI silk floss

F = 114 sage green

Au Ver à Soie, Soie d'Alger stranded silk

G = 5113 antique mauve

The Thread Gatherer Silk'n Colors stranded silk

H = silvered celery

YLI silk ribbon 4mm (3/16") wide

I = 1m (39 1/2") no. 158 dk pink

J = 1.6m (1yd 27") no. 163 med dusky pink

Vintage Ribbons hand dyed silk ribbon 4mm (3/16") wide

K = 50cm (19 1/2") pine needles

Colour Streams hand dyed silk ribbon 4mm (3/16") wide

L = 1.3m (1yd 15") no. 5 antique rose

No. 8 crewel needle

No. 10 crewel needle

No. 18 chenille needle

No. 22 chenille needle

EMBROIDERY KEY

All thread embroidery is worked with one strand unless otherwise specified.

Dark stem stitch roses

Centre = I (colonial knot)

Inner petals = J (stem stitch)

Outer petals = L (stem stitch)

Light stem stitch roses

Petals = L (stem stitch)

Centre = L (colonial knot)

Spider web roses = L (spider web rose)

Small roses = L (colonial knot - running stitch combination)

Clusters of ribbon knots = L (French knot, 2 wraps, colonial knot)

Rosebuds

Centre = I (twisted detached chain)

Side petals = L (ribbon stitch)

Sepals = K (ribbon stitch), C (fly stitch, straight stitch)

Tip = C (straight stitch)

Stems = C (stem stitch)

Violets

Petals = A (granitos), G (fly stitch, straight stitch)

Centre = E (colonial knot)

Forget-me-nots

Centre = E (colonial knot)

Petals = B (colonial knot)

Leaves

Large leaves = H (fly stitch, smocker's knot)

Small leaves = F (detached chain, fly stitch)

Sprays of knots = D (2 strands, colonial knot, French knot, 1 wrap)

~ Bluebirds ~

BY WENDIE YOUNG OF VICTORIA

Delicate climbing roses are entwined into a heart shape. A precious little bluebird, singing a beautiful love song, is sitting upon a tendril while a second bluebird is happily stretching its wings.

THIS DESIGN USES

Back stitch, Bullion knot, Bullion loop
Colonial knot, Fly stitch, Granitos
Satin stitch, Stem stitch, Straight stitch

REQUIREMENTS

Threads & Needles
See this page.

Supplies
10cm (4") embroidery hoop

PREPARATION FOR EMBROIDERY

See the liftout pattern for the embroidery design and page 70 for instructions for transferring the design.

EMBROIDERY

See the opposite page for the step-by-step instructions for working a satin stitch leaf.

Use the milliner's needle for the roses and rosebuds and the sharp needle for all other embroidery.

Work the bluebirds and leaves with the fabric in the hoop.

Order of work

Stems, tendrils and leaves

Embroider the stems and tendrils first, except for the tendril the top bird is sitting on. This is worked after the bird has been completed. All the stems and tendrils are worked with very tiny stem stitches.

Stitch all the leaves next, working the larger ones in satin stitch and the smaller ones with 3 - 4 tiny straight stitches of varying lengths.

Roses

Using the darker shade of plum thread, work the centre of each rose with a bullion loop.

Embroider two bullion knots for the inner petals, placing the smaller knot at the top of the rose. Change to the lighter shade of plum and stitch the outer petals.

Rosebuds

Stitch the centre two bullion knots in the darker shade of plum. Change to the lighter shade and work a bullion knot on each side for the outer petals. Overlap them slightly at the base.

Change to the olive thread and embroider 4 - 5 straight stitches, overlapping them at the base for the calyx. Add 2 - 3 straight stitches near the top of each bud for the calyx tips. Finish the calyx with a granitos of three tiny straight stitches. Work a straight stitch for the stem.

Bluebirds

Using the ecru thread, embroider the face in satin stitch. Work the breast with the carnation thread and the lower body with the ecru thread.

Stitch the cap, wings and tail using the blue thread. Embroider the tips on the tail. Partially outline the wings with stem stitch.

Embroider the tendril over the tail of the upper left bluebird. Finally, stitch the eyes, beak and feet using the black silk floss.

THREADS & NEEDLES

Gumnut Yarns 'Stars' stranded silk

A = 073 vy lt carnation

B = 193 lt ripe plum

C = 195 med ripe plum

D = 349 dk denim blue

E = 677 med olive

F = 991 ecru

YLI silk floss

G = black

No. 12 sharp needle

No. 9 milliner's (straw) needle

Embroidery Key for Bluebirds

All embroidery is worked with one strand of thread.

Stems, tendrils and leaves

Stems = E (stem stitch)

Tendrils = E (stem stitch)

Leaves = E (satin stitch, straight stitch)

Roses

Centre = C (bullion loop, 14 wraps)

Inner petals = C (2 bullion knots, 16 - 18 wraps)

Outer petals = B (5 bullion knots, 14 wraps)

Rosebuds

Centre = C (2 bullion knots, 10 wraps)

Petals = B (2 bullion knots, 14 wraps)

Calyx = E (straight stitch, granitos)

Stem = E (straight stitch)

Bluebirds

Face = F (satin stitch)

Cap = D (satin stitch)

Lower body = F (satin stitch)

Breast = A (satin stitch)

Wings = D (satin stitch)

Wing outline = F (stem stitch)

Tail = D (satin stitch)

Tail tip = F (straight stitch)

Eyes = G (colonial knot)

Beak = G (straight stitch)

Feet = G (fly stitch)

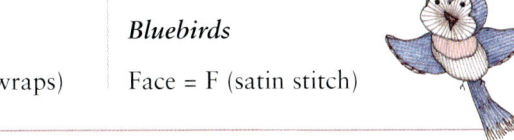

Step-by-step satin stitch leaf

To create these lustrous leaves the satin stitches are carefully angled towards the tip.

1. Work running stitches inside the leaf shape to secure thread without a knot. Bring thread to front at A.

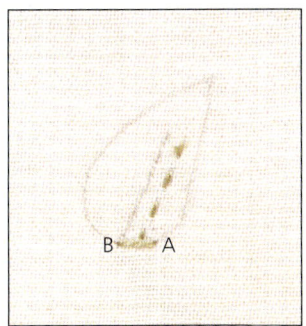

2. Take the thread to the back at B, on the centre vein.

3. Bring the needle to the front at C, beside the first stitch and just above A.

4. Take the thread to the back at D, just above B.

5. Following the leaf shape, continue working satin stitch up one side of the leaf vein.

6. Slightly fan the satin stitches until the first half of the leaf is filled.

7. Continuing on from the tip, work second half as a mirror image of first half.

8. End off the thread on the back of the fabric. **Completed satin stitch leaf.**

~ Lattice Heart ~

BY KRIS RICHARDS OF SOUTH AUSTRALIA

Soft, blushing roses and blue forget-me-nots climb around a pale pink lattice heart. Violet daisies and tiny buds complete the design.

THIS DESIGN USES

Bullion knot, Detached chain French knot, Stem stitch, Straight stitch

REQUIREMENTS

Threads & Needle
See this page.

Supplies
12.5cm (5") square of quilt batting

PREPARATION FOR EMBROIDERY

See the liftout pattern for the embroidery design and page 70 for instructions for transferring the design.

EMBROIDERY

All embroidery is worked with the milliner's needle.

Order of work

Roses
Work the two centre petals of the roses using the darkest shade of pink. Stitch the next round of petals in the medium pink. Work the outer petals using the palest pink or soft white thread. On most of the roses, embroider the outer petals around the lower edge and sides only.

Rosebuds
Embroider four rosebuds near the centre 'dip' of the heart and three at the lower tip. Stitch one bullion knot for the centre petal in all buds except one. Work two bullion knots side by side for the centre of this rosebud. Embroider the outer petals with two bullion knots. Add a straight stitch to the tip.

Leaves
Scatter detached chain leaves around the roses and rosebuds. Stitch some leaves with each green thread so the colours mix.

Forget-me-nots
Embroider the yellow French knot centres first. Add 3 - 8 blue-violet French knots for the petals.

Partial daisies and small buds
Scatter violet detached chain petals around the roses, referring to the photograph as a guide for placement. Nestle French knot buds among the larger flowers.

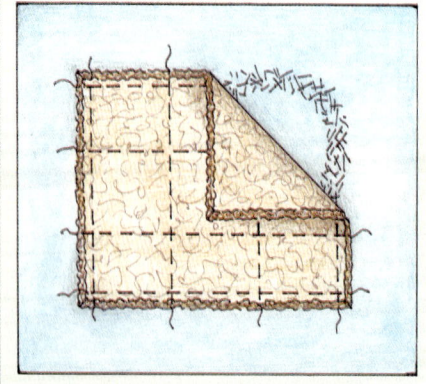

DIAG 1

Lattice
Tack the piece of batting to the back of the fabric *(diag 1)*. Stitch the lattice in stem stitch. Carefully trim the batting close to the heart shape.

THREADS & NEEDLE

Madeira stranded silk

A = 0807 lt antique violet
B = 0812 med shell pink
C = 0813 lt shell pink
D = 0815 ultra lt shell pink
E = 0901 lt blue-violet
F = 1408 avocado green
G = 1510 lt green-grey
H = 2208 lt old gold
I = 2401 soft white

No. 9 *milliner's (straw) needle*

EMBROIDERY KEY

All embroidery is worked with one strand of thread.

Roses
Centre = B (2 bullion knots, 6 wraps)
Inner petals = C
(2 - 3 bullion knots, 10 wraps)
Outer petals = D or I
(2 - 5 bullion knots, 12 wraps)

Rosebuds
Centre = B (1 - 2 bullion knots, 6 wraps)
Outer petals = C
(2 bullion knots, 10 wraps)
Tip = B (straight stitch)

Leaves = F and G (detached chain)

Forget-me-nots
Petals = E
(French knot, 1 wrap)
Centre = H (French knot, 3 wraps)

Partial daisies = A (detached chain)

Small buds = I and D
(French knot, 2 wraps)

Lattice = D (stem stitch)

~ Sweethearts ~

BY JULIE GRAUE OF SOUTH AUSTRALIA

Two dainty bluebirds hold the ends of a satin stitched ribbon which gently folds into a heart. Beautiful pink roses and soft white bullion flowers are evenly spaced along the length of the ribbon.

REQUIREMENTS

Threads & Needles
See this page.

Supplies
12.5cm (5") embroidery hoop

PREPARATION FOR EMBROIDERY

See the liftout pattern for the embroidery design and page 70 for instructions for transferring the design.

EMBROIDERY

Use the no. 7 milliner's needle to work the bullion roses and daisies. The no. 9 milliner's needle is used for all other embroidery.

Embroider the bluebirds and the ribbon in the hoop.

Order of work

Ribbon

Outline the ribbon in split stitch. Using the photograph as a guide for stitch direction, work satin stitch over the split stitch. Work three dark pink French knots at each end of the ribbon.

Bluebirds

Stitch the two bluebirds in shadow work. Embroider a French knot for the eye of each bird and two straight stitches for each beak.

Roses

Stitch the roses, beginning with the centre petal in the darkest pink. Work three inner petals in the medium pink, followed by five outer petals in the lightest pink.

Daisies

Embroider the bullion loop petals, keeping the ends as close as possible to the middle. Stitch a French knot in the centre of each flower.

Leaves

Embroider detached chain leaves around the roses and daisies.

Tiny buds

Add 2 - 4 pink French knots around the roses and 1 - 3 mauve French knots near the daisies.

THREADS & NEEDLES

Madeira stranded silk

A = 0807 antique violet
B = 0812 med shell pink
C = 0813 lt shell pink
D = 0815 ultra lt shell pink
E = 0901 lt blue-violet
F = 1510 lt green-grey
G = 1912 med beige-brown
H = 2207 vy lt old gold
I = 2401 soft white

No. 7 milliner's (straw) needle
No. 9 milliner's (straw) needle

THIS DESIGN USES

Bullion knot, Bullion loop
Detached chain, French knot, Satin stitch
Shadow work, Split stitch, Straight stitch

EMBROIDERY KEY

All embroidery is worked with two strands of thread unless otherwise specified.

Ribbon = E
(1 strand, split stitch, satin stitch)

Dots = B
(1 strand, French knot, 1 wrap)

Bluebirds
Bird = E (1 strand, shadow work)
Beak = G (1 strand, straight stitch)

Eyes = G
(1 strand, French knot, 2 wraps)

Roses
Centre = B (bullion loop, 10 wraps)
Inner petals = C
(3 bullion knots, 10 wraps)
Outer petals = D
(5 bullion knots, 10 wraps)

Daisies
Petals = I (bullion loop, 15 wraps)
Centre = H (French knot, 2 wraps)
Leaves = F (1 strand, detached chain)

Tiny buds
Pink buds = C (French knot, 1 wrap)
Mauve buds = A
(French knot, 1 wrap)

STEP-BY-STEP DARK STEM STITCH ROSE

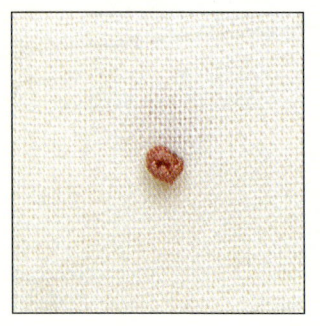

1. Centre. Thread the ribbon into a no. 22 chenille needle and bring it to the front. Work a tight colonial knot.

2. Work 6 - 7 colonial knots around the first one, keeping them very close together and pulling each one firmly.

3. Petals. Change ribbon and use a no. 18 chenille needle. Work a round of stem stitches as close as possible to the centre. Overlap the first stitch with the last.

4. With the lightest ribbon, work a second round of stem stitches. Work stitches very close to the previous round. **Completed rose.**

STEP-BY-STEP RIBBON ROSEBUD

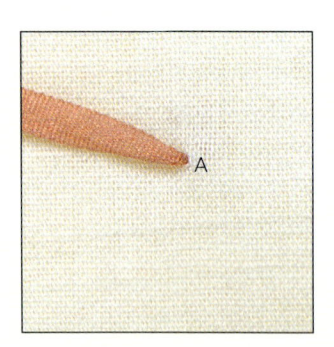

1. Centre. Thread a no. 22 chenille needle with the ribbon and bring it to the front of the fabric at A.

2. Work a twisted detached chain for the centre of the bud. End off the ribbon on the back of the fabric.

3. Side petals. Change to a lighter coloured ribbon. Bring the ribbon to the front at B, slightly to one side of the base of the bud.

4. Work a ribbon stitch across the bud to C.

5. Work a second petal from D to E in the same manner.

6. Sepals. With the green ribbon, work two ribbon stitches in the same manner. Make them slightly shorter than the petals.

7. Change to the green thread and the no. 10 crewel needle. Work a fly stitch around the base of the bud.

8. Work a straight stitch from the base to halfway along the bud. Work two straight stitches of different lengths from the tip. **Completed ribbon rosebud.**

FROM WEDDING FOLKLORE

A BRIDE IS NOT SUPPOSED TO WEEP BEFORE MARRIAGE, BUT SHE MAY DO SO TO HER HEART'S CONTENT AFTER THE ACTUAL CEREMONY - AND THUS PROVE THAT SHE IS NO WITCH, AS THE LATTER COULD ONLY SHED THREE TEARS FROM HER LEFT EYE!

ANGELS OF LOVE

BY SUSAN O'CONNOR OF VICTORIA

*In this heavenly embroidery design,
a flowing blue-violet ribbon entwines two whimsical cupids,
clasping a circlet of fragrant flowers.*

The finished design measures
4.2cm x 16.5cm wide
(1 5/8" x 6 1/2").

REQUIREMENTS

Threads & Needles
See page 78.
Supplies
Tracing paper
Sharp lead pencil
20cm (8") embroidery hoop

PREPARATION FOR EMBROIDERY

See the liftout pattern for the embroidery design.

Transferring the design

Using a black pen, trace the design onto tracing paper. With the right side of the fabric facing, place the fabric over the tracing so it is in the desired position. Ensure the straight grain of the fabric is aligned with the placement lines on the tracing. Pin in place to prevent movement. Using the lead pencil, trace the design. Trace the cupids and ribbons and mark the centres of the roses, daisies and forget-me-nots with dots.

EMBROIDERY

See page 79 for step-by-step instructions for open fishbone stitch.

Use the milliner's needle for the bullion knots and the sharp needle for all other embroidery. All embroidery is worked with the fabric in the hoop, except for the bullion knots.

ANGELS OF LOVE

Order of work

Cupids

Outline the body and face of each cupid in split stitch. Fill each section with satin stitch, covering the split stitch. Add the shading to the bodies and cheeks with satin and straight stitches worked over the previous stitching. Next, work the back stitch outlines. Embroider closely packed French knots for the hair.

Using the white thread, outline the wings in split stitch. Completely cover the wings with vertical satin stitches. Change thread colour and embroider back stitch around each wing section. Work open fishbone stitch along the upper two sections of the lower wings. Repeat the procedure in the three lower sections closest to the cupids' bodies.

Ribbon

Outline each section of the ribbon in split stitch. Fill each section with satin stitch, completely covering the split stitch outlines.

Circlet of flowers

Embroider the bullion roses first. For each one, work a bullion loop at the centre. Surround the centre with three bullion knots for the inner petals and then work five bullion knots for the outer petals.

Stitch the rose leaves and daisy petals with detached chains. Work the petals of the forget-me-nots next, using five knots for the complete flowers and 2 - 4 knots for the partial flowers. Finally, add gold French knots to the centres of the daisies and forget-me-nots.

THIS DESIGN USES

Back stitch, Bullion knot
Detached chain, French knot
Open fishbone stitch, Satin stitch
Split stitch, Straight stitch

THREADS & NEEDLES

Madeira stranded silk

A = 0807 antique violet
B = 0812 dk shell pink
C = 0813 shell pink
D = 0815 vy lt shell pink
E = 0901 lt blue-violet
F = 1510 lt Jacobean green
G = 1910 lt mushroom
H = 1912 med beige-brown
I = 2207 vy lt old gold
J = 2208 lt old gold
K = 2401 soft white

No. 10 milliner's (straw) needle
No. 12 sharp needle

EMBROIDERY KEY

All embroidery is worked with one strand of thread unless otherwise specified.

Cupids

Body and face = G
(split stitch, satin stitch)

Body and face markings = C
(satin stitch, straight stitch)

Outlines = C and H (back stitch)

Hair = J (2 strands, French knot, 1 wrap)

Wings = K
(split stitch, satin stitch)

Wing outlines = I (back stitch)

Wing markings = I
(open fishbone stitch)

Ribbon = E
(split stitch, satin stitch)

Roses

Centre = B
(2 strands, bullion loop, 10 wraps)

Inner petals = C (2 strands, 3 bullion knots, 10 wraps)

Outer petals = D (2 strands, 5 bullion knots, 10 wraps)

Leaves = F (detached chain)

White daisies

Petals = K
(detached chain)

Centre = J (French knot, 1 wrap)

Forget-me-nots

Petals = A
(French knot, 1 wrap)

Centre = J (French knot, 1 wrap)

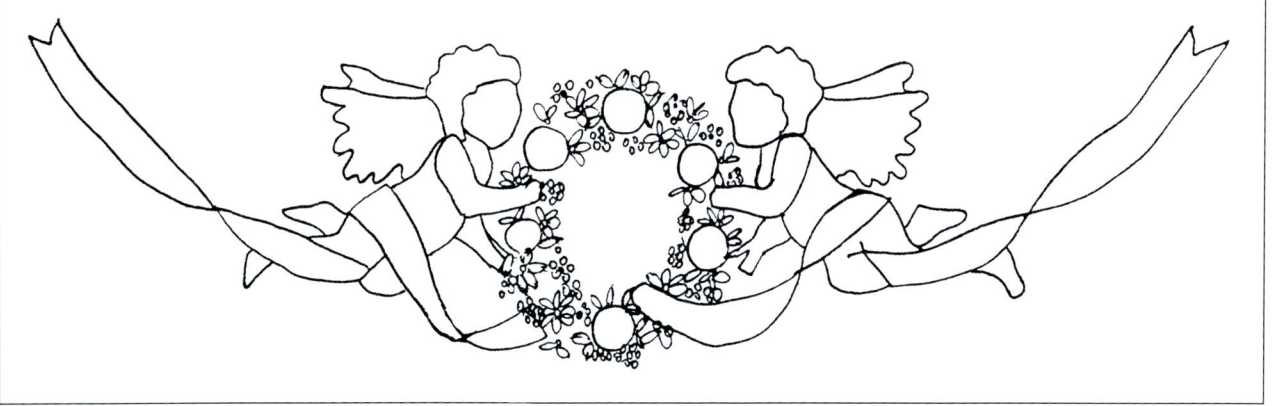

*Love to faults is always blind, Always is to joy inclined,
Lawless, winged, and unconfined, And breaks all chains from every mind.*
WILLIAM BLAKE

STEP-BY-STEP OPEN FISHBONE STITCH

1. Bring the thread to the front at A, on the left hand side near the top of the shape.

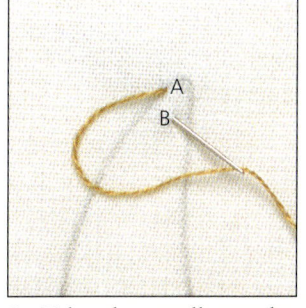

2. Take the needle to the back at B, diagonally below and just to the right of the middle of the shape.

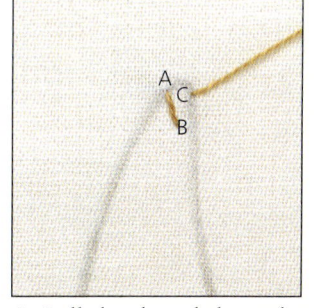

3. Pull the thread through. Re-emerge at C, on the right hand side directly opposite A. Pull the thread through.

4. Take the needle to the back at D, just to the left and slightly below B. This stitch crosses the previous stitch.

5. Pull the thread through. Re-emerge at E, a short distance below A.

6. Pull the thread through. Take the needle to the back at F. This stitch crosses the previous stitch.

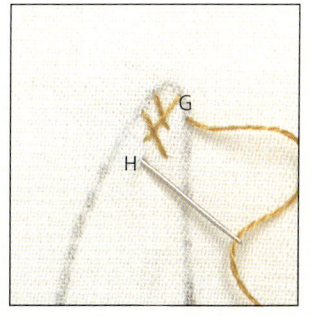

7. Pull the thread through. Re-emerge at G and take the needle to the back at H.

8. Continue working stitches in the same manner until shape is filled. End off thread. **Completed open fishbone stitch.**

*Thank you so very much to the many dedicated people
who have made this book possible.*

THE CONTRIBUTORS
*Elina Akselrod, Helen Eriksson, Julie Graue, Di Kirchner, Jane Nicholas,
Susan O'Connor, Carolyn Pearce, Kris Richards and Wendie Young*

THE EDITORIAL AND DESIGN TEAM
*Kathleen Barac, Margie Bauer, Victoria Bauer, Sue Gardner,
Lynton Grandison, Sarah Kent, Lizzie Kulinski, Jenny McWhinney,
Heather Moody, Naomi Nelson, Susan O'Connor, Joy Peters,
Wendy Sousophat and Vivienne Twelftree*

*Special thanks to Heidelberg Cakes, Philicia Antiques, Betrothed,
Quigley Antiques, Al Rue Farm, Jo Barber, Sarah Abbey*

PHOTOGRAPHY *Andrew Dunbar*

REPROGRAPHICS *van Gastel Graphics*

PRINT *Custom Press*

PUBLISHER *Margie Bauer*

Proudly produced and printed in South Australia

ISBN 0-9579069-2-7

Copyright © 2002 Country Bumpkin Publications

All rights reserved. No part of this book, text, photographs or illustrations may be reproduced
or transmitted in any form or by any means print, photoprint, microfilm, microfiche, photocopier,
internet or in any way known or as yet unknown, or stored in a retrieval system, without written
permission obtained beforehand from Country Bumpkin Publications.
Readers are permitted to reproduce any of the items/patterns in this book for their personal use,
or for the purposes of selling for charity, free of charge and without prior permission of the Publisher.
Any use of the items/patterns for commercial purposes is not permitted without
prior permission of the Publisher.

INSPIRATIONS BRIDAL
Liftout Pattern

SERENITY

by Di Kirchner of South Australia
For colour photos and full details, see pages 10 - 11.

REQUIREMENTS
For full details, see pages 10 & 11.

PREPARATION FOR EMBROIDERY
For full instructions, see page 10.

EMBROIDERY
For full instructions, see page 11.

CUTTING OUT
Where pattern pieces are not provided cut the pieces according to the measurements below.

White voile
Cut two, each 4.5cm x 82cm wide (1 ¾" x 32 ⅜")

CUTTING LAYOUT
White Voile
1. Base for embroidery
2. Garter

CONSTRUCTION
All seam allowances are 5mm (³⁄₁₆") unless otherwise specified. The shaded areas on the following diagrams indicate the right side of the fabric.

1. Attaching the beads
With wrong sides together, fold one piece of voile in half along the length and finger press. Unfold. To find the centre, fold again across the width and finger press. Measure out 6.5cm (2 ½") from the centre. Using the lead pencil, mark the fold line with a small dot at this measurement. Continue making small dots at 4cm (1 ½") intervals along the fold line until reaching the end. Repeat the procedure on the remaining half of the piece *(diag 1)*. On the right side of the fabric, secure a pearl bead to each marked dot.

Pin and tack in place. Attach the second piece of lace edging to the opposite side in the same manner *(diag 2)*.

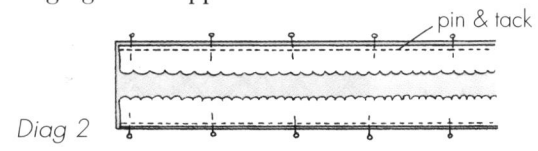

Diag 2

With right sides together, place the second piece of voile over the first. The lace edging is sandwiched between the two layers of fabric. Stitch along each long side following the stitch line. Turn the garter through to the right side and press.

3. Making the casing
Form a casing for the elastic by sewing along the length of the tube 7mm (⁵⁄₁₆") in from each finished edge of the voile *(diag 3)*.

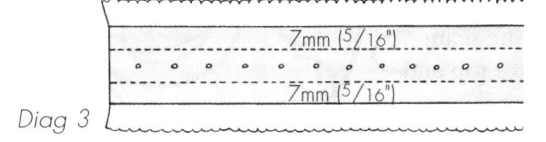

Diag 3

4. Inserting the elastic
Attach the elastic firmly to one end of the garter. Using a bobbin or safety pin, thread the elastic through to the other end, gathering the fabric at the same time. Attach the elastic firmly to this end of the garter *(diag 4)*.

Diag 4

5. Completing the garter
With right sides facing, overcast the

DESIGNS OF THE HEART

EMBROIDERY DESIGNS
For colour photos and full details, see pages 68 - 76.

placement guide

RIBBON ROSE HEART
EMBOIDERY KEY

- ⊙ Dark Stem Stitch Rose
- ○ Light Stem Stitch Rose
- ◎ Spider Web Rose
- ⊕ Small Rose

Ribbon Rose Heart
by Carolyn Pearce of New South Wales

Sweethearts
by Julie Graue of South Australia

PEACE

by Kris Richards of South Australia
For colour photos and full details, see pages 30 - 35.

REQUIREMENTS
For full details, see pages 32 & 34.

PREPARATION FOR EMBROIDERY
For full instructions, see page 32.

EMBROIDERY
For full instructions, see pages 32 - 35.

CUTTING OUT
Where pattern pieces are not provided cut the pieces according to the measurements below.

Organza
Bag: cut one, 35cm x 130cm wide (13 ¾" x 51 ¼")
Sash: cut one, 27cm x 135cm wide (10 ⅝" x 53")
Gently tear the fabric, rather than cutting with scissors, as it leaves a feathered edge which does not show as much from the right side when the project is finished. The diagonal ends will need to be cut with scissors.
Tab: cut one, 12cm x 5cm wide (4 ¾" x 2")

CUTTING LAYOUT

Organza
1. Bag
2. Sash
3. Tab

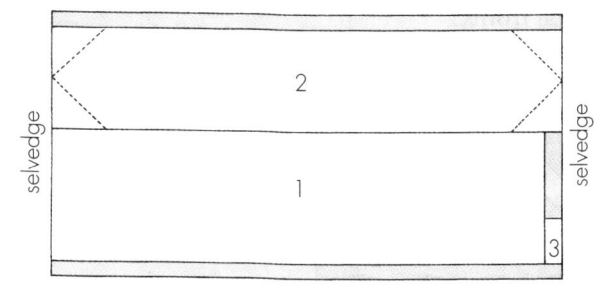

CONSTRUCTION
All seam allowances are 1cm (⅜") unless otherwise specified. The shaded areas on the following diagrams indicate the right side of the fabric.

1. Preparation
Remove all traces of the fabric marker and take out the grid of tacking over the embroidery. Leave in the tacking around the edges. Place the fabric face down on a well padded surface and press.

2. Side seams
With right sides together, fold the tacked fabrics in half. Pin and stitch each side. Neaten the seams with a machine zigzag or overlock stitch *(diag 1)*.

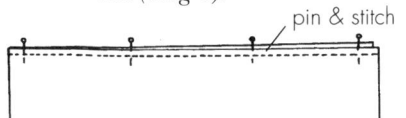

Measure down 22cm (8 ⅝") from the top of the bag at the centre back and pin the tab to the bag *(diag 3)*.

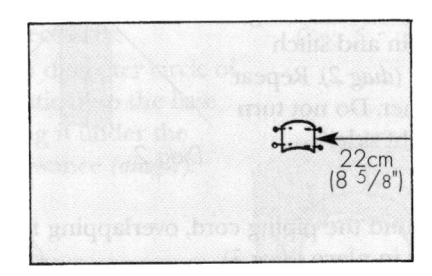

Diag 3

Secure with small hand stitches. Attach the lower edge of the tab in the same manner.

4. Hemming the upper edge
At the upper edge, turn under 1cm (⅜") and press. Turn under a further 11.5cm (4 ½") and press. Hand stitch the hem in place ensuring your needle goes through the organza and moiré along the folded edge *(diag 4)*.

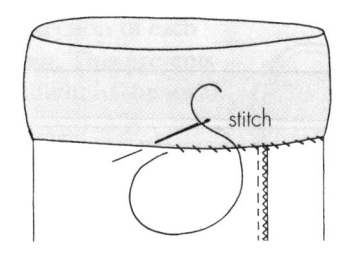

Diag 4

4. Sash
With right sides together fold the sash piece in half along the length. At one end, fold down the corner to form a diagonal fold *(diag 5)*.

Diag 5

Press and cut along the fold line. Repeat at the other end. Stitch across one end and approximately halfway along the long edge. Leave a 10cm (4") opening and then continue stitching along the long edge and across the remaining end *(diag 6)*.

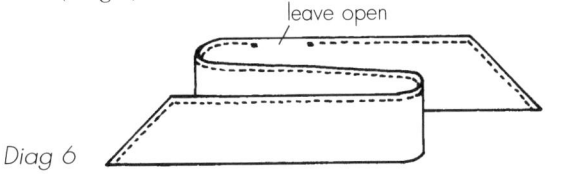

Diag 6

Turn to the right side and press, pressing under the seam allowance along the opening. Hand stitch the opening closed. Press.

5. Finishing the bag

ROMANCE

by Di Kirchner of South Australia
For colour photos and full details, see pages 12 - 13.

REQUIREMENTS
For full details, see page 13.

EMBROIDERY
For full instructions, see page 13.

CONSTRUCTION
All seam allowances are 1cm (3/8") unless otherwise specified. The shaded areas on the following diagrams indicate the right side of the fabric.

1. Attaching the lace
Roll a narrow double hem on each end of the lace and hand stitch. Beginning and ending 6mm (¼") from each end and with right sides together, pin the lace along one long edge of the fabric strip with the lace heading 4mm (3/16") from the raw edge. Tack in place just below the lace heading *(diag 1)*.

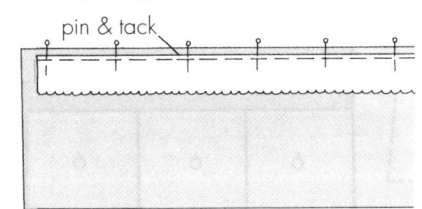

Diag 1

With right sides together, fold the fabric in half along the length. Machine stitch along the line of tacking. Remove the tacking. Turn through to the right side and press. Top stitch 2mm (1/16") from the seam *(diag 2)*. On one end of the fabric tube, turn in 6mm (¼") and press. Hand stitch the opening closed.

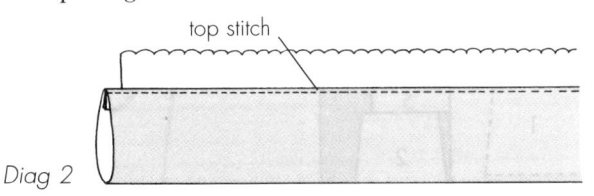

Diag 2

3. Forming the horseshoe
Trace the horseshoe template onto the cardboard or plastic and cut out. Cut two pieces of wadding using the horseshoe template. Sandwich the cardboard or plastic between the two pieces of wadding. Using matching machine thread, overcast the two pieces of wadding together around all edges *(diag 3)*. Carefully feed the fabric onto the horseshoe shape. Close the opening in the same manner as the first end. Arrange the

Diag 3

4. Attaching the ribbon loop
Cut a 40cm (15 ¾") length of ribbon. Fold under 6mm (¼") at one end. Place the folded end onto the back of the horseshoe, positioning it at the centre of one end. Hand stitch in place *(diag 4)*. Attach the remaining end of the ribbon to the other end of the horseshoe in the same manner.

Diag 4

5. Attaching the ribbon to the front
Cut a 40cm (15 ¾") length of white satin ribbon. Fold the ribbon in half to find the centre and mark the centre with a pin.

At the centre front mark the halfway point between the upper and lower edges of the voile with the lead pencil. From this point, continue making marks at 4cm (1 ½") intervals until 4cm (1 ½") from each end of the horseshoe *(diag 5)*.

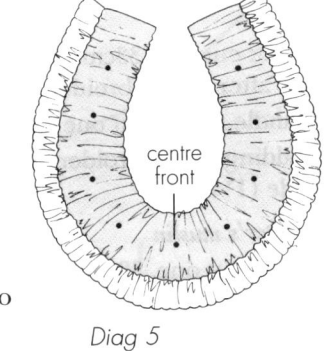

Pin the centre of the ribbon to the centre front mark on the horseshoe. Hand stitch in place. Attach the ribbon in place at each marked dot along the horseshoe and at the ends, trimming and turning under. Embroider the horseshoe following the instructions on page 13.

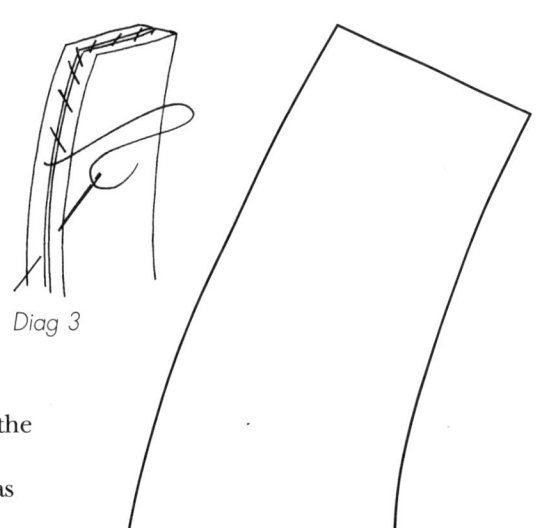

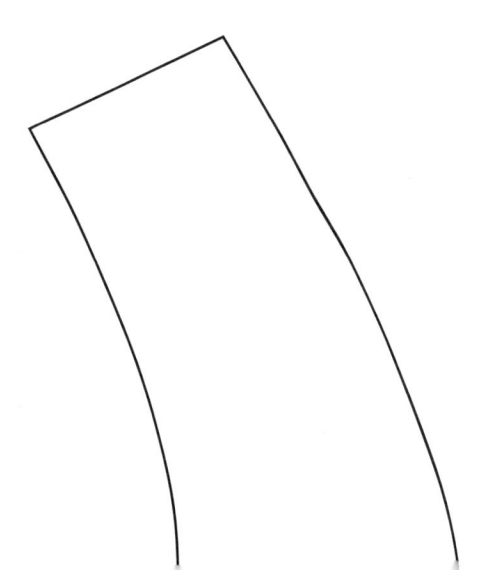

Diag 5